C000216396

Best wishes
from all at Investec

Investec is proud to support Make-A-Wish Ireland

IRELAND IN BRICK AND STONE

The Island's History in its Buildings

IRELAND IN BRICK AND STONE

The Island's History in its Buildings

Richard Killeen

Gill & Macmillan

Gill & Macmillan
Hume Avenue, Park West, Dublin 12
with associated companies throughout the world
www.gillmacmillanbooks.ie

© Richard Killeen 2012
978 07171 5360 2

Index compiled by Cover to Cover
Design and print origination by O'K Graphic Design, Dublin
Printed by Printer Trento, Srl, Italy

This book is typeset in 12/16 pt Bembo.

The paper used in this book comes from the wood pulp of managed forests. For every tree felled, at least one tree is planted, thereby renewing natural resources.

A CIP catalogue record for this book is available from the British Library.

1 3 5 4 2

CONTENTS

INTRODUCTION

This book is a series of narrative and interpretative essays. It looks at aspects of Irish history, prompted by a selection of fifty buildings or other man-made artefacts. The buildings are presented roughly in the chronological order of their significance so as to maintain a general sense of narrative flow. All but three of the buildings are still extant. One of the artefacts is not a building at all, but a landscape.

This is not an attempt to write a history of Ireland. It is, of its nature, selective. The selection is mine alone. Although it cannot be comprehensive it attempts to strike a balance between the obvious and the neglected. This is more easily done as we move towards the modern era, when there is a greater availability of source material and of published work. The closer we approach the present, the more dense the historical landscape becomes and the greater the choice of subject matter one has.

None the less, there are essentials to the Irish story that cannot be ignored. It would be a nice undertaking to write about the Irish past without any reference to politics or religion, and while it would not be a completely false exercise it would hardly fool anyone for long. There are dozens of quotidian concerns that make up the stuff of history but which get marginalised by grand narratives: diet, dress, sanitary arrangements, transport, money, childbirth, plagues, shelter, communication, housekeeping, literacy, dentistry, shopping. The list goes on. Some of these subjects are touched on at points in this book, although the reader will be pleased to learn at the outset that the author has resisted the temptation to dilate on either dentistry or childbirth, on the grounds of profound ignorance.

One may think of this book, therefore, almost as a series of personal snapshots. It is predicated on the simple and obvious proposition that history is about the transformation of land and landscape by human volition. The changes thus wrought become decisive when we cannot imagine — I mean that literally — the world before the transformative event. To select from the list above, our modern imaginations find it almost impossible to envisage a world without electricity, flush toilets and department stores. Yet these are all inventions and developments of the last 200 years. The series of events and locales described in this book cover a period of more than 1,500 years. It is one thing to know that most of our ancestors — and not just our remote ancestors — had to do without these and other marvels. It is quite another to *imagine* how they actually lived.

This is the hardest task for any historian, to set aside the automatic assumptions which constitute the silent grammar of modern life when fumbling for an understanding of a world in which these things were not merely absent, but had not yet been dreamed of or imagined.

History too is a fairly modern discipline. As an academic subject, it is effectively a nineteenth-century invention, and it runs in parallel with the development of European nationalism. National grand narratives still form the backbone of history writing, pushing the quotidian stuff to one side, but also furnishing readers with a structure and a context for the partial recovery of the past. Without that structure, we simply don't have the vocabulary to attempt the task at all.

This book is a modest attempt to look at occasional aspects of ordinary social life without losing sight of that larger narrative. Like all compromises, it may fall between two stools. That is for you, dear reader, to decide.

RK, Dublin, February 2012

SLANE FRIARY

he remains of Slane Friary, on a hill overlooking the modern village of Slane in Co. Meath, can be clearly seen from the road as one approaches the village from Dublin. This is the main road to Derry and western Ulster. At Slane it crosses the River Boyne just a few miles to the west of Brú na Bóinne — the bend of the Boyne — where the river turns in a U-shape before resuming its eastward journey to the sea at Mornington. Within the U lie the Neolithic sites of Newgrange, Knowth and Dowth, the first of these being one of the true wonders of Ireland.

As old as the Egyptian pyramids, Newgrange is a passage tomb, a burial site. It is 11 metres high and over 80 metres in diameter, with a corbelled roof that has kept the interior dry for nearly four millennia, this in a country with abundant rainfall. A series of gutters carry rainwater to the margins of the tomb, where it runs off harmlessly. The tomb is aligned to the rising sun on midwinter day, for on that day and that day alone a lightbox over the entrance admits the rays of the sun, just breaking the horizon to the east, to flood the full length of the entry passage and to strike the back wall of the central burial chamber. The unknown pastoral people who built this and other extraordinary structures long antedated the Celts.

The Celtic peoples who occupied Ireland from about 300 BC and created a common linguistic culture throughout the island also established themselves in this lush river valley and its environs. This is rich limestone land, perfect for the pastoral rural economy of the Celts, as it had been for all the peoples that preceded them and whom they had obliterated from history. The royal site of Tara — seat of the kings of the southern Uí Néill — lies just 15 km to the south west. This was a provincial centre of some importance, although its later inflation into the seat of the high kings of Ireland was a nationalist whimsy: there was no such centralised authority in Celtic Ireland. Tara had been a site of military and strategic importance in pre-Celtic times, for like Cashel in Munster it commands a stunning view of the flat country all around and is therefore a formidable defensive position. It has evidence of human settlement from as far back as the 3rd millennium BC.

For all the early inhabitants of Ireland, this was a landscape worth possessing. So it is no surprise that the story of Christianity in Ireland starts here, albeit with what is certainly a fable. According the legend, St Patrick converted the local king at the hill above Slane to Christianity by showing him a shamrock and explaining that the trefoil leaves in the one plant represented an image of the unity of the Trinity.

According to the ballad, St Patrick was a gentleman — he came of dacent people. True. He is for the most part a figure of mystery, although the shadow of the real person is discernible. And this is for a reason: that he is the first figure in the history of the island to leave us a written record of any kind. In his case, he has left us a record of himself, a kind of displaced autobiography.

Two fragments are all we have, but they are undoubtedly the work of his hand. So, who was he? He was the son of a Romanised British family, born in the early fifth century, who had been captured by Irish piratical raiders and sold into slavery. His family were Christian, like all the late Roman elite, metropolitan and provincial alike. Having eventually escaped back to Britain, he dreamed that he was being recalled to Ireland to evangelise the island for Christ.

He was probably not the first Christian missionary in the country but he was certainly one of the most potent. His mission was confined to the northern half of the island: the southern half contains no verifiable Patrician sites. And the two documents he has left us? The first, and more important, his *Confessio*, is the text from which we can patch together the outline of his life. The second, the *Letter to Coroticus*, is a bitter protest against the depredations of a British chieftain whose troops came ashore in Ireland and slaughtered newly evangelised Christians, an outrage that Patrick might have felt with particular keenness given his own earlier experience at the hands of the Irish.

So this is the ambiguous man who stands before the sub-king above Slane, some time in the early fifth century, and convinces him of the Trinitarian version of Christianity. Or doesn't. Almost certainly, this is the purest myth and there is not a shred of evidence in support of it. Which is important: because the point of Patrick is not that we can prove that he did this or that, or even that he was the national evangelist, but that he was the first living, breathing human being on the island of Ireland of whom we have a secure record, however tentative. Before him, all is conjecture, heroic myth and uncertainty. Here is flesh and blood: a real person.

The French have a marvellous phrase, *les lieux de mémoire*: the sites of memory. Slane is Ireland's first such site, not because of what happened here (it didn't) but because of how it has been remembered. When Patrick converted the king — so the story goes — it was Eastertide, the most sacred moment in the Christian calendar. And here, on the hill above Slane in the early fifth century, he lit the first Paschal Fire ever seen in Ireland: the light upon a hill that kindled a tradition still living today.

The Hill of Slane is also the site of the earliest documented mention of a round tower, that most distinctive of early Christian structures, in the Irish annals. No trace of it remains, it having been burned by the Vikings.

The story of Patrick and the Paschal Flame may be a myth, but it is an enabling one. On this site, important since pre-history, occurs the first narrative event in the history of Irish Christianity. And even if that narrative was fiction, it was no less powerful for that. Here, not long after Patrick, St Erc founded a monastery which subsisted for the best part of a millennium until the Franciscans established a friary in the early sixteenth century, just a generation or so before friaries and monasteries got it in the neck from Henry VIII. The church there finally closed as a place of worship in the early eighteenth century, and it is the ruins of this late medieval/early modern ecclesiastical complex that you see from the road as you drive north towards Slane.

GALLARUS

The far western end of the Dingle peninsula is a heart-stopping landscape. At Dunmore Head, just as the coast road reveals the stunning view of the Blasket Islands, you are at the most westerly point in Europe: the next parish to America. It is like standing at the outer arms of Sydney Harbour and looking across the Pacific in the knowledge that beyond that vast expanse of blue there is nothing between you and Santiago in Chile. For Santiago, read Boston, Massachusetts. Actually, if you follow lines of latitude, read the Strait of Belle Isle that separates the northern tip of Newfoundland from Labrador. But let's not get too literal.

This is a harsh and unforgiving land, for all its beauty. It is stony, arid and utterly remote. In every sense, it is as far from the lush plains of Co. Meath as it is possible to be on the same small island. For most of human history, it has been accessible by land only with the greatest difficulty. To this day, access — the demand for which has been ramped up by tourism — is still confined to narrow, single-carriageway roads. A narrow-gauge railway, itself never commercial, went only as far as Dingle and closed in the 1950s. And here we are 20 km west of Dingle. Traditionally, the sea was the highway here.

Blasket Sound, the whip of water that separates the mainland from the Great Blasket, is a vicious funnel through which the entire North Atlantic flows. In calm summer weather, it looks like an idyllic millpond. In winter, it can be a cauldron. Here, in September 1588, three ships of the Spanish Armada, having made a heroic anti-clockwise circumnavigation of the British Isles on the return journey to Spain, met their end during an apocalyptic autumn storm. Eight years earlier, in 1580, a papal force of 1,000 infantry, sent in support of the Counter-Reformation rebellion of the Earls of Desmond — whose lands encompassed the peninsula — landed at Smerwick Harbour on the more sheltered northern shore under Mount Brandon. There they built a fort, known then and ever since as *Dún an Óir*, the fort of gold. They bore papal letters absolving the Irish lords from allegiance to Queen Elizabeth I and calling for a religious war to secure Catholicism in Ireland. This was the great ideological fault line of the age. It was all or nothing for both sides, which helps to explain the horrors of the war.

The papal force was trapped at Smerwick by Lord Grey de Wilton, the chief governor, and massacred. The English response to the Desmond rebellion was pitiless: famine, together with wholesale slaughter of people and livestock. War *à l'outrance* was the means employed and it reduced the entire earldom, which stretched from this remote western fastness to the rich plains of central and eastern Munster, to a barren, starving shambles.

A few kilometres inland from Dunmore Head to the south and from *Dún an Óir* to the north, more or less in the centre of the narrow peninsula, stands the intriguing corbelled oratory of Gallarus. It is tiny. It looks for all the world like an upturned boat. It dates from around 1000 AD and is one of the best-preserved early Christian buildings in the country. Its remoteness and its diminutive size may account for the fact that what we see now is what its builder saw when he finished it.

The oratory of Gallarus is completely unmortared. The stones are laid each upon the other with such overlapping precision that it is bone dry inside and has remained so for more than a thousand years in one of the wettest locations in the northern hemisphere. This ancient corbelling technique had been used since Neolithic times, and had been employed in many of the great pre-historic burial sites. It is perhaps no surprise that such an enduring construction technique should have been deployed so successfully here three millennia after it had first been perfected on the island.

It is speculated that the principal function of Gallarus Oratory was as a way station

— a place of prayer — on a pilgrimage route, possibly a seaborne route to the Camino de Santiago de Compostella. Smerwick nearby would have furnished a safe haven along this otherwise forbidding coast.

Gallarus is also redolent of the anchorite tradition in the early Irish Christian church. Because early Christian Ireland had no towns to serve as foci for dioceses, the structure of church government differed from the norm of Latin Christianity. The Irish church was monastic in structure: the great early monasteries served as proto-towns and proto-universities. But they never acquired the full sinews of urban life, nor did they develop into universities in the continental sense, as at Bologna and Paris.

Part of the monastic enterprise was a consistent search for purity of spirit, a rejection of the material and a retreat to remote places in pursuit of a spiritual life cleansed of luxury or wealth. The reform movement in the early Irish church known as the *Céile Dé* (the Companions of God) were especially remembered for their zealous ascetic excesses, but they were part of a tradition, not altogether at the margin of the early church, that reappeared on a regular basis. Extremes of fasting, the denial of music and an idealisation of the early desert fathers drove such rigorists towards remote and barren places like the western edge of the Dingle Peninsula. An even more celebrated and dramatic location was on the Great Skellig Rock, a vast triangular sea stack 16 km off shore, clearly visible to the south in clear weather.

These were the locations of the Irish 'desert fathers', echoing the anchorite ascetics of the early Eastern Church, whose huge influence in early Christianity was later eclipsed by the eminence of Rome in the west. Indeed, the Irish word 'dysert', which occurs in a number of place names around the island, is cognate with the Latin *desertus*. The excesses of the ascetics were often lampooned by more orthodox and worldly monastic writers. Not the least of these lampoons is the *Navigatio Sancti Brendani Abbatis*, otherwise the celebrated Voyage of St Brendan. A work of fiction, it has been read (and mis-read) as the story of an actual voyage, although some of the details are so plausible that it may be based on the lost account of a voyage that was actually accomplished.

Although it was written as a theological tract intended to satirise the ascetics, its popular fame came from its metaphor of the voyage and spawned the myth that St Brendan sailed from Brandon Creek, just below Gallarus, and discovered America in the sixth century. He may or may not have: we shall never know. In the 1970s, the adventurer Tim Severin established that it could have been done using sixth-century naval technology. It was a possibility — and it is as logical to believe that St Brendan sailed from here and reached North America centuries before the Vikings or the Basques or Columbus as it is to dismiss it all as whimsy.

CLONMACNOISE

The monastery of Clonmacnoise — one of the most dramatically sited in Ireland — stands on the eastern shore of the River Shannon just below the town of Athlone. Its location is no accident. This is the point at which the principal east–west route in ancient Ireland crossed the Shannon, itself the great north–south artery. (It can never be repeated often enough that water-borne transport was easier than overland until the proper metalling of roads in the early nineteenth century.) It is also close to the provincial boundary between Leinster and Connacht — the river being a very obvious part of that boundary — and as a consequence it drew patronage from both provinces. A number of Connacht kings are buried there.

The foundation is usually dated to the 540s, barely a century after St Patrick. Nothing survives from the early centuries; the buildings were almost certainly timber-built and perishable. Only when stone structures are first erected, from the tenth century, does the site assume the rough appearance with which we are familiar.

The spread of monastic settlements went hand in hand with the spread of literacy, grounded in the centrality of the Bible. Gradually, the influence of literate scholars —

most of them initially in holy orders — embraced the secular world of the law. Clerical influence on the law was very marked from the eighth century. The older, customary law was gradually but decisively replaced by written codes. Moreover, it changed in nature, becoming more severe. Traditionally, the unwritten law had permitted material restitution even in some cases of murder. Clerical influence — clearly drawing from Biblical precedents — was much harsher. Kings were now encouraged to eschew milder forms of sanction in favour of capital punishment for capital crimes.

This is one of the less obvious consequences of early Irish monasticism. There are numerous examples of capital punishment. At Clonmacnoise, in the early eleventh century, a thief who had attempted to steal some of the monastery's treasures was unceremoniously hanged by the community. He had been handed over to them by the local king.

The early monasteries were centres of learning and piety, but they were also prone to human rivalries and jealousies. Clonmacnoise saw itself, and was seen, as a rival to the ecclesiastical primacy of Armagh. As early as the seventh century, the bishop of Armagh complained of Clonmacnoise appropriating foundations, previously under the protection of Armagh, that had been abandoned due to a devastating plague. In this, the diffuse nature of ecclesiastical jurisdiction — with no agreed central authority or first among equals, despite Armagh's claims — echoed the absence of a central political authority. No high king; no archbishop. Armagh enjoyed the prestige of its Patrician connection, but not the enforceable primacy that it asserted over the rest of the Irish church.

The Viking depredations of the late eighth and early ninth centuries affected Clonmacnoise as surely as they did other wealthy monastic targets. It was raided in 835, just as the foundation was recovering from an even more devastating raid two years earlier at the hands of the king of Munster, who killed half the community and destroyed its buildings by fire. The Vikings were back in 845, attacking monastic sites all along the Shannon, and once again Clonmacnoise was torched, although the Gaelic annals (or at least a version of them composed centuries later as a propaganda vehicle for Brian Ború) gleefully report the wife of the Viking chieftain draping herself in suggestive and lewd poses on the high altar.

The monastic enclosure that lies in a largely ruinous state on the banks of the river began to take permanent shape with the erection of the first stone buildings in the early tenth century. These were the smallest and largest churches on the site, respectively Temple Ciarán — reputed to be the burial place of the saint — and the so-called cathedral. This latter term should not confuse us: it was a small church (albeit it the principal one within the enclosure, ergo the inflated name) typical of Irish sites, not at all the large, imposing structure one immediately thinks of in a comparative European context. Over time, other small temples were added, as well as two round towers and three high crosses.

The high crosses, of which the Cross of the Scriptures is the finest, were parables in stone, representations in relief of Biblical and scriptural scenes, often employing animal symbols. In this, their purpose was similar to that of the stained-glass windows in Gothic cathedrals: offering a version of Christian instruction to an illiterate laity. The round towers were basically campaniles — bell towers — although they also served as treasuries, boltholes and lookout posts. These latter functions were secondary to a round tower's primary purpose. The mistaken belief that they were mainly places of refuge is anachronistic, if only because they were ill-suited for that purpose, being natural flues and therefore death traps for those inside if a fire was set at the bottom. But the further error in all this proceeds from the fact that the round towers date from a period when Viking raids on monastic sites had either abated or stopped altogether.

Round towers are Ireland's most distinctive contribution to early medieval European architecture. The two at Clonmacnoise, the smaller of which is well preserved, are by no means the most dramatic examples in the country, although their location is unrivalled for its drama.

Following the arrival of the Normans after 1169, Clonmacnoise gradually declined in fortune. Although it had developed as a proto-town, with tradesmen and other skilled laity dependent on it and available to it, the twelfth-century ecclesiastical reforms — which established the four provinces and a European-style diocesan system — bypassed it. As a result, it lost the patronage of kings and aristocrats which had sustained its wealth and prestige for seven centuries. It finally fell victim to the fury of the Reformation: an English army sailed down river from its garrison at Athlone and laid it waste in 1552.

In short, Clonmacnoise had been a place of some importance in Ireland for just under a thousand years. It seems utterly remote in time from us now, in its semi-ruinous state. But it has only been like this for half the time it was in its pomp.

4

REGINALD'S TOWER

The term Viking refers to groups of Scandinavian people principally from the south and west coasts of what is now Norway, and the Jutland peninsula to the south across the Skagerrak. These people, in possession of their lands from ancient times, had probably been part of successive patterns of migration by Germanic tribes across the Great Northern Plain of Europe, which offered few natural obstacles to such migration.

Quite what impelled the Vikings to their sudden, violent and energetic expansion overseas from the eighth century is uncertain. There may have been population pressures, which would have been particularly severe in Norway with its rocky coastal valleys trapped and surrounded by impassable mountains on the landward side. The combination of limited and poor land together with the unforgiving northern climate would have made such habitats especially vulnerable to population growth, with any surplus population impelled to shift for itself. The gradual development of the proto-kingdoms of Norway and Denmark in the early Viking period may also have caused tribal groups alienated from the move towards centralised kingdoms to seek their fortunes elsewhere.

The Vikings appear for the first time off the Irish coast in 795 and attacked the wealthy monastery on Lambay island, just north of Dublin Bay. They were raiding in search of loot and treasure and in this they were not alone, for native Irish raiders did not scruple to emulate their example. Undefended monasteries and their riches made a tempting target. For almost half a century, these Viking depredations continued, with the Norse the principal presence on the east and south coasts while the Danes pushed farther inland in their shallow-draughted longboats.

This so-called 'hit and run' period ended in 841 with the establishment of a proto-settlement, known as a *longphort*, on the banks of the Liffey. A *longphort* was a defensible enclosure for shipping which offered adequate berthage and easy access to the open sea. The establishment of the settlement marks the foundation date of the city of Dublin. The towns of Cork, Limerick, Wexford and Waterford all followed either side of 900 CE, each of them of Viking foundation. Interestingly, the Vikings fared worse in Ulster, where the Uí Néill had the measure of them.

Waterford dates from the first twenty years of the tenth century. The name is Norse, *Vadrefjord*, meaning the inlet of the ram. Indeed, the magnificent harbour — fed by three major rivers of the south-east of Ireland, the Barrow, Nore and Suir — looks on a map vaguely like a ram's horn. At any rate, it is the finest natural harbour and safe haven in Ireland. It is no surprise that the Vikings sent their longships there and founded a settlement.

Reginald's Tower, named for its alleged Viking builder, is the oldest surviving civic building in Ireland. It dates from about 1000 CE. It is almost certainly the first building in Ireland — and beyond doubt the oldest to have survived intact — to have been constructed using mortared stone. Its original function was military, standing as it does at the eastern salient of the old town walls where they touched the quay. It therefore commanded the seaborne approach to the settlement upriver.

As in the other urban settlements they started, the Vikings were displaced by the Normans in Waterford. The city prospered for centuries on shipbuilding and trade. It was well positioned for the wool and meat trades to Flanders and to the Low Countries generally, as well as to the west of England. In later centuries, it had a vigorous commerce with the West Indies and with North America. Its staple cargoes included butter, salted beef and pork, wine and cod. Bristol was a key connection, both as a port of destination and transit, but Waterford ships traded as far afield as Lisbon and Cadiz.

In modern times, Waterford became best known for its eponymous crystal. But the city's origins are unmistakably Viking, although nearly all traces of their foundational presence have disappeared. Reginald's Tower is the conspicuous exception to that rule. On the contrary, the Norman — and by extension, Old English — inheritance is still palpable.

Ireland as we know it is unimaginable without the Viking contribution. All the island's urban life starts with them and for that alone they are an indispensable presence in the Irish past. They have had a bad history — all that raping and pillaging — not least because the history was written by the raped and the pillaged. But towns and cities are essential building blocks of civilisation. They provide a focus for commerce, trade, fine architecture, schools of learning, specialisation of function, civic and religious display. They are forcing houses for talent and human energy. One of the great differences between those parts of Europe outside the ambit of the Roman Empire and those within was that the empire was essentially a network of towns, all diminutive Romes linked by a kind of invisible mental thread to the eternal city.

That was why the post-imperial Christian church was organised on a diocesan basis, with each diocese centred on the greatest town in its region. In Ireland, which had no towns before the Vikings, the church's organisational structure was monastic and did not come into line with standard European practice until the thirteenth century.

So, whatever destruction the Vikings wrought on Gaelic Ireland, they also started a process of urban development that was absolutely fundamental to the subsequent history of the island. Had it not been them, it would have been others. But those others would, like the Vikings, almost certainly have been invaders, foreigners; for Gaelic Ireland had shown no potential for significant urban development. This was unusual in early medieval Europe. Towns often thought of as classic colonial impositions — like the Hanseatic towns and cities along the eastern Baltic — were in fact developed versions of pre-existing if less sophisticated urban centres.

There were no such centres of distribution and exchange in Gaelic Ireland. The Vikings were the *fons et origo* of Irish urbanity. And for that, we owe honour to their memory, so splendidly extant in stone on the waterfront in Waterford.

5

CASHEL

T he Rock of Cashel is a dramatic limestone promontory standing proud above the flat, fertile lands of Co. Tipperary. From time immemorial, it has been a fortified position from which its possessors enjoy an unrivalled view of the countryside all around.

From the start of recorded history, it was the principal fortress of the kings of Munster. For most of the medieval period, the dynasty known as the Eóganachta dominated the province. Their dominance lasted until 976, when the small sub-kingdom of Dal Cais in what is now east Co. Clare suddenly began one of the more improbable adventures in all of Irish history.

It was the story of one remarkable man, Brian mac Cennétig, known ever after as Brian Ború. He succeeded his murdered brother as king of Dal Cais and within two years he had overthrown the Eóganachta kings and installed himself as king of Munster. By 1000, he was the effective ruler of the southern half of Ireland, having partitioned the island by agreement with Mael Seachnaill, king of the southern Uí Néill, who had previously claimed the high kingship of Ireland from his base at Tara in Co. Meath. This claim was as empty as all that had preceded it: the partition arrangement was, if nothing else, proof of that. But for Brian, it had been a stunning progress, from obscure provincial sub-king to effective warlord of half the island in a single lifetime.

Nor was he finished. In 999, he broke the truce and defeated a coalition of Mael Seachnaill and the Dublin Vikings and occupied Dublin for more than a month. In 1001, he launched himself against the southern Uí Néill. Mael Seachnaill found himself abandoned by allies, including the northern branch of his dynasty. His failure to compel his allies, even his own kin, is a stark demonstration of the limitations of kingly power in Gaelic Ireland. If an outstanding figure like Mael Seachnaill could not do it, who could?

Mael Seachnaill acknowledged Brian's overlordship in 1002. In the following years, Brian pressed ever further north. In 1005, he secured the support of the see of Armagh, a key advance. This was the occasion that first caused him to be called *Imperator Scottorum*, or emperor of the Irish. The following year, he made a royal tour of Ulster without any opposition, although the stubborn little kingdom of Cenél Conaill in the very west of the province held out on him until 1011. In every year following the submission of Mael Seachnaill in 1002, Brian had felt required to assert himself in Ulster, making his royal progress and taking local hostages as an earnest of the local rulers' submission to his power.

He was the nearest thing Gaelic Ireland had seen, or was ever to see, to a true high king. But this much abused term obscures as much as it illuminates. Brian was not a king in any common understanding of the word. He did not administer a territory from a secure, permanent capital. His legal writ did not run throughout the territory he claimed. He did not have any central revenue-raising powers. These were all characteristics of early European kingdoms: none were present in Brian Boru's Ireland.

And to be fair, even in Europe, they were for the most part characteristics of future, not present, royal kingdoms in the first decade of the eleventh century.

His hold on power was precarious. In 1011, a coalition of Leinster kingdoms and the Dublin Vikings rose against Brian's overlordship. The issue was settled in 1014 at the Battle of Clontarf with a victory for Brian, but one that cost him his life as well as that of his fifteen-year-old grandson. His successors — taking the family name O'Brien in honour of his memory — were unable to emulate his achievements. Gaelic Ireland reverted to its previous pattern of local kings and contested boundaries. Brian's kingdom of Munster did not hold together, breaking into two major units: Desmond and Thomond, respectively the southern and northern halves.

In 1101, the Rock of Cashel had been granted to the church and in due time it became the centre of the southern archdiocesan province, when the ecclesiastical reforms of the twelfth century were put in place. In the meantime, in 1127 one Cormac McCarthy, king of Desmond, commissioned the chapel on the Rock that has ever after borne his name.

It is an example of the Hiberno-Romanesque style then coming into vogue. The common European architectural style known as Romanesque developed from about 1000 and is characteristic of the next two centuries or so before the rise of Gothic. Unlike its successor style, it was characterised by rounded rather than pointed arches and a monumentality that drew in part on imperial Roman models and in part from Byzantium, at that time at the apogee of its cultural prestige.

The Irish variation of this common European theme is interesting for what it lacks as well as for what it contains. Compared to one of the great Romanesque cathedrals on the continent, the Irish versions lacked all monumentality. As before, Irish churches remained small, unassertive structures until the arrival of the Normans. But the mere fact that Romanesque had made its way to Ireland — although the pulse beat weakly — was significant. The kinds of external influences that had brought the Vikings to the island and would soon bring the Normans were not lost on the Gaelic kings.

Cormac MacCarthy wished his chapel to mimic the prevailing architectural fashion on the continent, although the building does contain some features characteristic of more traditional construction techniques. It was therefore, like the style it typifies, a hybrid. It is lavishly decorated, with evidence of continental craftsmen having contributed to it, and appears to have been intended as the king's private chapel. It was consecrated in 1134.

A more substantial cathedral was later added on the Rock, but it was burned twice: once by Garret Mór Fitzgerald, the effective ruler of Ireland in the late fifteenth century, and then by Lord Inchiquin, the notorious arsonist, during the confused wars of the 1640s. After the first of these depredations, it is told that King Henry VII demanded to know what Garret Mór thought he was doing in burning the cathedral, to which he replied that he was sorry but he had thought that the archbishop was inside!

The apse of Angoulême cathedral in France, an example of exuberant European Romanesque.

6

CLONFERT CATHEDRAL

W hen we think cathedral, we think 'big'. The word comes from the Latin *cathedra*, a chair or — by extension — a throne. Its original definition referred specifically to a chair for women but it later acquired the further meaning of a professorial chair, as in a university. This latter meaning was further displaced to form the root of the word that describes the principal church of a diocese, where the bishop has his seat or throne.

The great cathedrals of Europe, from Durham to Istanbul, are huge symphonies in stone attesting the power and wealth of the Christian church. They are also declarations of political intent, because the church was a secular as well as an ecclesiastical power. Indeed, the distinction between the two was blurred — to put it gently. In the chaotic vacuum left by the collapse of the Roman Empire in the west, the Latin church and its monarch — the Pope in Rome — were the sole focus of legitimate authority for centuries.

Only after 800 AD, with the rise of Charlemagne, was a secular authority established which realised effective political and military control over a large territory. But the integrity of that territory did not survive Charlemagne's death — the Brian Boru problem on a continental scale — and his empire split into the kingdoms of east and west Francia, the remote antecedents of Germany and France.

The gradual re-establishment of political and secular authority in Europe in the centuries after Charlemagne led to the formation of the Holy Roman Empire, which can be dated to the mid-tenth century. This was one of history's great misnomers, for this empire was really a confederation of German princes in alliance against Slavs and Magyars. Indeed, the full title — the Holy Roman Empire of the German People — was more revealing. When Charlemagne had been crowned in Rome by Pope Leo III, the Pope had knelt before the new emperor. Leo's successors very decidedly declined to follow suit, and in the early centuries of the Holy Roman Empire there was a blatant tussle for supreme authority between pope and emperor in which the greatest papal triumph was achieved at Canossa, in the Italian Alps, where Pope Gregory VII, having excommunicated the emperor, left him standing in the snow for three days begging forgiveness before restoring him to the bosom of the church.

These exercises in power and main force were echoed in the great European cathedrals. We normally think of these as built in the Gothic style. This is fair enough, for many of those that most readily come to mind — Notre Dame, Chartres, Cologne, Salisbury — are indeed among the great triumphs of Gothic. But there are cathedrals and churches that antedate the Gothic era, and the prevailing style in those centuries — roughly from 600 to 1000 — was Romanesque. This was based on the Roman semi-circular arch, rather than the pointed arch that distinguished Gothic; rectilinear towers rather than spires; and a repetition of the rounded form in the apse.

There are spectacular examples of Romanesque ecclesiastical architecture all over western Europe. The cathedral at Pisa is one of the best known, as is that of Durham in the north-east of England — although Durham's roof vaulting anticipates and marks the mutation to the Gothic style. Yet in Ireland we have almost nothing in the

Romanesque, just a few examples such as Cormac's chapel — and the western doorway of Clonfert cathedral.

The monastery on this site was founded by St Brendan the Navigator in 563 AD and his remains are buried here. Nothing survives of the original foundation. The present church — it seems an exaggeration to call such a modest building a cathedral, mentally conflating it with Pisa and Durham — is thought to date from the tenth century. The doorway is a later addition, and may date from 1179, when a synod convened there. Modest it may be, but this is the highest achievement of Romanesque architecture in Ireland.

The rounded doorway, with its highly elaborated decorations in six orders, is surmounted by a triangular hood within which the rounded arch theme is continued in decorative miniature. Some of the decoration is a later addition, for repairs were carried out to the church in the early fifteenth century, but for the most part this is the most authentic and integral example of Romanesque that Ireland possesses.

The architecture that dominated Europe for at least four centuries if not longer is barely represented at the continent's western margin, and then only in fragments. These centuries are properly thought of as the golden age of Irish Christianity, the age of the great missionaries and *peregrini* who re-evangelised the continent after the collapse of the western empire. The traffic was mostly one way. The insular Celtic church, with its distinctive structure of ecclesiastical governance based on monasteries rather than dioceses (for want of towns), was remote from the prevailing continental norm. This is reflected in the littleness of its buildings, their modesty and lack of pomp, their indifference to prevailing fashion. Perhaps these are more meritorious Christian virtues than the worldly swagger of continental Romanesque, but they serve to remind us yet again that pre-Norman Ireland was a faraway place, and remote from the centre of the larger culture of which it was nominally a part.

The incursions of the Vikings — the first external force to establish itself in Gaelic Ireland — have left us little in the way of surviving buildings and there is no sense in which they effected an architectural connection with the continent, despite their foundation of towns. That had to await the coming of the Normans. In the juvenile version of Irish history, choked on its own self-pity, the arrival of the Normans in the late twelfth century — just before the building of the western doorway at Clonfert — marks the great tragic fracture in the Irish story, the moment of violation and dispossession.

It is also the moment that Europe finally came to its western island and one of the best days the island ever saw.

7

CHRIST CHURCH CATHEDRAL

A t Christmas 1171, Henri FitzEmpress Plantagenet took the sacrament of communion in the Church of the Holy Trinity in Dublin. He was king of England, duke of Normandy and count of Anjou. His wife, Aliénor d'Aquitaine, brought to the marriage her ancestral duchy, so that Henri headed a state that stretched from the Scottish borders to the Pyrenees and included most of the western half of France. In England, he was sovereign. He owed homage to the king of France in respect of his territories there, but these were so much more extensive than the land controlled by the king — who only ruled directly in the Île de France — that there was little doubt as to who was the mightier prince.

We know him as Henry II of England, which he was. But he was so much more, and the claim that he and his successors made on their French lands would be the source of wars for the next 300 years. The matter was only settled in 1453 at the battle of Castillon near Bordeaux with the final victory of the French crown over the English, leaving only the redoubt of Calais in English hands — and even that went a hundred years later.

Henri was French. He and his successors as kings of England spoke French, as did all the new nobility put in place by the Norman conquest. They were a foreign elite, colonial masters who ruled from the top down through military might and their own legal code. They disdained the Anglo-Saxon language and culture; they maintained their linguistic difference — and their stubborn connection to France, to whose very crown they were to lay claim in time — until 1399. In that year, Henry IV became the first king of England whose mother tongue was English.

In 1166, Henri was on campaign in Aquitaine when he received a visit from Diarmait Mac Murchada, who had been extruded from his kingdom of Leinster in the east of Ireland and forced to flee abroad. He sought help to recover his kingdom. Henri was sympathetic but could not spare any troops. He did, however, however, give him letters authorising him to raise troops back in Britain. In return, Diarmait pledged to hold Leinster as Henri's vassal and to offer his daughter's hand to whatever military leader might be found in Henri's lands.

Diarmait duly raised troops in Norman Wales, returned and recovered some of his lands in 1167, was reinforced by more Norman troops that landed in 1169 and an even more formidable force in 1170. Its leader was Richard fitzGilbert, deposed Earl of Pembroke, known to history as Strongbow. It was he who claimed the hand of Diarmait's daughter Aoife. Strongbow and his men captured Dublin in that same year.

Indeed, so successful were they that Henri — for whom Ireland was a distraction — was obliged to take control. He feared that Strongbow would establish an independent kingdom in Ireland.

This was no paranoid fantasy on the king's part. Once the Normans had arrived in force, in the summer of 1070, they brought a level of military power unlike anything seen before in Ireland. Their two key military resources were mounted and armoured knights and the longbow. The former, on their huge horses, were irresistible. A disciplined Norman cavalry charge was a terrifying experience. Likewise, the longbowmen could engage and devastate an enemy at distance. The quick military successes of the Normans in Ireland were no accident.

Henri landed at Waterford in October 1171 with the largest and most formidable army ever seen in Ireland. The whole armada comprised 400 ships. This was a serious invasion force. Its purpose was to secure the feudal allegiance, not just of the Norman beachhead, but of the Gaelic kingdoms as well, to the crown of England. This is the moment at which that crown inserts itself into the history of Ireland. It is also the reason that Henri was receiving communion that Christmas in the church that was to become Christ Church cathedral. It was the first time he had felt able to take the sacrament since the murder, at his instigation, of Thomas à Becket, the archbishop of Canterbury, almost a year previously.

Christ Church had been founded by the Vikings about 150 years earlier. It stood on the east–west ridge that runs parallel to the Liffey, rising ground that offered an obvious defensible position just above the anchorage on the river. It was the chief church of the little town and has retained that position to the present day. The Normans rebuilt it and after many centuries of neglect, it assumed its modern appearance in the 1870s, when the architect G.E. Street 'restored' it with all the bull-necked self-assurance of the Victorian era, so that the present building is in effect a nineteenth-century confection. That said, it does retain some elements of the medieval fabric. This is especially true of the crypt, the largest in the British Isles. The money for this exercise was furnished by the distiller Henry Roe, just as the money for a similar makeover of St Patrick's cathedral down the way was supplied by Sir Benjamin Lee Guinness, the brewer.

Strongbow is buried in Christ Church. He ended his days in 1176, having succeeded his father-in-law Diarmait as lord of Leinster. In 1189, the year of Henri's death, Strongbow's daughter Isabella married William Marshall. Ten years later, William assumed the earldom of Pembroke from King John (Jean sans Terre), the title that Strongbow's father had held but which Henri had denied to the son.

The coming of the Normans is the moment at which continental Europe begins to impact on the island. Norman military and legal culture, its systems of municipal governance, its church reforms and its overbearing architecture all changed the face of the country permanently. This was a European colony, whose presence was mediated through the crown of England. Its effect has not always been benign but it has been indelible.

8

CARRICKFERGUS

arly in 1177, John de Courcy, one of the new Norman knights in Ireland, headed north from Dublin with twenty-two cavalry and 300 infantry. He pushed through the Gap of the North, the Moyry Pass through which both the road and railway line that connect Dublin and Belfast run today. It is one of the few natural access points to the province of Ulster, whose necklace of hills and lakes girdles the province and presents a natural barrier to incursion from the south.

Despite his modest numbers, de Courcy demonstrated in the most emphatic fashion the superiority of Norman arms by winning two battles against Gaelic chieftains in the area known as Lecale, near Downpatrick. The Norman cavalry, protected by mail armour and riding in stirrups — two accessories unknown to the Irish — proved irresistible. Not that de Courcy had it all his own way: he did not win all his battles and was vulnerable to ambushes in countryside that was strange to him but familiar to the Ulstermen.

None the less, he established himself. And he built. Stone castles, by far the biggest human artefacts yet seen in Ireland, were the Normans' key means of securing and defending their position in conquered territory. This was as true in Ireland as in Wales or Sicily, where there was a Norman kingdom from 1130 to 1194. And none was more impressive or more intimidating than the great castle de Courcy built at Carrickfergus, on the shore of Belfast Lough, to secure the northern end of his coastal territory which now encompassed much of modern Co. Down.

In 1180, he married the daughter of the king of the Isle of Man, and her dowry included a fleet of ships. By keeping the sea to his back, de Courcy had the means both to trade and *in extremis* to escape. The latter option was not needed. Carrickfergus castle and others that he strung around the margins of his new territory were impregnable to attack by the Ulstermen.

Carrickfergus is the anglicised version of *Carraig Fhearghais*, meaning the rock of Fergus, the eponym being a local sixth-century king of Dal Riada. This was a seaborne Gaelic kingdom, with its twin poles in north-east Ulster and south-west Scotland. It had existed from about the fifth century when Gaelic warriors from Ulster made the crossing over the narrow passage of the North Channel to create a sister kingdom in Argyll (from the Gaelic *Oirear Gael*, shore of the Gaels). Scotland is very close: the Mull of Kintyre is clearly visible from the top of Torr Head in north Antrim. In the classic way of the ancient world, the sea was a highway rather than a barrier: it was easier for Ulster to colonise part of western Scotland than to form a connection with the rest of Ireland to the south. Here was an enduring theme in the province's history.

The castle that de Courcy built at Carrickfergus was formidable even by Norman standards: it stands alongside de Lacy's castle at Trim and King John's Castle in Limerick as the most assertive of their kind. The inner keep or *donjon* has walls nine feet thick. Its four storeys rise 90 feet above the rock on which it rests. This was the warlord's untouchable citadel and de Courcy established what was in effect a palatinate jurisdiction in these conquered lands, minting his own coins and dispensing justice through his barons.

All this lasted until 1199, when de Courcy fell foul of the new king John (Jean sans Terre). The king encouraged a younger son of Trim Castle, Hugh de Lacy, to make war on de Courcy. By 1205, de Lacy had won and was created earl of Ulster, while de Courcy was put to flight. He tried to recover his lands by launching a seaborne invasion force from the Isle of Man with help from Reginald, the Manx king, his brother-in-law. He failed.

The medieval earldom of Ulster was as much subject to the Gaelic re-conquest of the thirteenth and fourteenth centuries as other parts of the island previously subdued. Yet de Courcy's achievement was never wholly undone. Even in the darkest moments of the colony in the late Middle Ages, the toehold in Ulster that owed a formal allegiance to the crown held out. Although outside the Pale in the literal sense, the colonists still controlled the coastal marchland south of Belfast Lough as well as the great redoubt of Carrickfergus on its northern shore. It is no accident that, when the plantation schemes for Ulster were first mooted in the sixteenth century, these lands were the first to be planted. The private scheme sponsored by Sir Thomas Smith in what are now Cos Antrim and Down proved to be a short-term failure but a long-term success — so much so that they were never part of the official Plantation of Ulster because they did not need to be.

The medieval earldom of Ulster was the farthest northern margin of the conquest, but its survival — however vestigial at times — provided a beachhead. It was at Carrickfergus that William of Orange landed in 1690 to settle one of the decisive quarrels of Irish history, one whose aftershocks are still felt. It was a marginal place, always vulnerable: the French under Admiral Thurot held Belfast Lough and environs for a week during the Seven Years' War in 1760 and in the next decade the American privateer John Paul Jones sailed a fleet into the Lough and laid about him without let or hindrance.

And yet, despite these external threats, the Presbyterians of Antrim and Down, the coastal counties nearest to Scotland and thus most heavily influenced by the Calvinism of the Scottish Kirk, also furnished the Ulster republican rebels of the 1790s. These were internal rebels, chafing at the effortless superiority and exactions of the eighteenth-century Anglican establishment from whom they were remote socially, temperamentally and theologically. They were defeated, and in their defeat discovered that however unpleasant the Anglicans, they were at least fellow Protestants. Thus was sown the germ of pan-Protestant solidarity, a hothouse flower that requires much nervous attention but one that is the basis of the modern unionist tradition in Ulster.

9

MELLIFONT

I n the very first year of the twelfth century, 1101, a council of the Irish Christian church met at Cashel. In the previous century, there had been a gradual movement towards church reform, intended to bring the insular church into a more orthodox communion with Rome in terms of liturgy, law and governance. The best evidence we have of this movement is a letter from the great reforming Pope Gregory VII (1073–85) to the king of Munster, which is the only known communication between the Papacy and anyone in Ireland for over 400 years. The long isolation of the Irish church was ending.

The process of reform begun at Cashel reached its full maturity half a century later at the Synod of Kells. It established the four Irish archdioceses that have survived to the present day, adding Dublin and Tuam to the existing Armagh and Cashel. Although named for Kells, the synod also met at the new Cistercian foundation at nearby Mellifont.

Mellifont stands on the northern side of the Boyne valley about half way between Slane Priory and the great monastery at Monasterboice, which holds two of the finest high crosses in Ireland. Mellifont was founded by St Malachy in 1142 on land granted to him by the local Gaelic lord. It was the first Cistercian house in Ireland.

Malachy had been a reforming archbishop of Armagh in the 1130s but his modernising efforts met with robust opposition from conservative clergy. Not the least of these was a sept whose kinsmen had had a stranglehold on appointments in the archbishopric of Armagh for almost two centuries, precisely the sort of nepotistic abuse the reformers were trying to tackle. Frustrated, he resigned and made his way to Rome, where he was appointed papal legate to Ireland. On both his outward and return journeys, he had visited the Cistercian abbey of Clairvaux, south-east of Paris near Troyes. Here, he left four of his followers to be trained as Cistercians. It was they who founded Mellifont, under Malachy's leadership, in 1142.

The Cistercians spread rapidly throughout Ireland during the rest of the century, and by its close Mellifont was joined by a further twenty-six foundations. The order reached its peak by the mid-thirteenth century and thereafter declined, with most foundations eventually being suppressed by Henry VIII in the 1530s. But although their glory days were relatively short, their contribution to medieval Ireland was exceptional. To understand why, it is necessary to look — as so often in Irish history — to the wider European perspective.

The Cistercian order had been founded in France in 1098. Its origins lay in the desire of its founders to restore the austerities of the rule of St Benedict, which had been diluted by the worldly riches of many Benedictine foundations. They were a product of the Gregorian church reforms, a series of changes in church governance associated with the name of Pope Gregory VII. The reforms were aimed at ending nepotism and clerical marriage (and marriage generally within the forbidden degrees of consanguinity), and at asserting both the primacy of the Pope over all temporal Christian kings and his position as absolute monarch of the Christian church.

The Cistercians fitted well into this new, rigorous regime. From their beginnings in northern France, they spread rapidly to England, Wales and the Scottish borders, following in the footsteps of the Norman conquest. Tintern Abbey, Fountains and Rievaulx in Yorkshire and Melrose in Scotland are all Cistercian houses. Moreover, they established themselves in other Norman kingdoms in southern Italy and Sicily. It was not simply a matter of following the Norman-French trail. The eastward drive of German-speaking merchants and adventurers towards Poland and the Baltic was also accompanied by a Cistercian presence. A monk from the Polish monastery of Lekno became bishop of Prussia in the early thirteenth century. Lithuania became the last territory in Europe to embrace Christianity, not doing so until the 1380s.

It was an age of expansion, conquest and colonialism throughout many parts of Europe. Ireland was no exception, nor in any way unique. And these expanding tribal and proto-national movements, of which the Norman-French and German examples are just the most prominent, were accompanied by evangelising missions (crusades in effect) in the eastern lands and ecclesiastical reform movements in western lands already Christian, the latter spearheaded by reforming orders like the Cistercians. It was no accident that the rapid expansion of the Cistercians in Ireland followed hard on the arrival of the Normans after 1170.

The Cistercians preferred relatively remote sites for their rigorous rule and were famed for their physical work ethic. They cleared uncultivated land and brought it under the plough. They developed a distinctive style of architecture for their monasteries, as we can see here at Mellifont. Typically, the monastery is arranged around a cloister (a fine surviving example of which can be seen at Jerpoint Abbey in Co. Kilkenny) with a church at the northern end and a chapter house at the southern. The combination of late Romanesque and early Gothic features is especially notable, although naturally the parts of each monastery that are of later date — as with the chapter house at Mellifont — display a greater Gothic emphasis. The finest surviving fragment at Mellifont — the octagonal lavabo or washing house — has the rounded arches so typical of the Romanesque style.

And fragments are all that remain, thanks to the state-sanctioned vandalism known as the Dissolution of the Monasteries. In a fit of destructive zeal, the sixteenth-century Reformers were not content to suppress religious houses — they had considerable justification for that, because of the luxury and corruption into which many had fallen — they felt the need to physically obliterate these beautiful places. Even in their ruinous state, the monasteries remain islands of civilised calm.

They were also, in their day, agents of colonialism. Just as the Normans represented the secular usages of continental Europe coming into Ireland, so the Cistercians and other orders (but especially the Cistercians) represented the spiritual analogue to the conquest. In one of history's ironies, it was here at Mellifont that Hugh O'Neill finally submitted to the crown of England in 1603 at the end of the Nine Years' war, the moment when Gaelic Ireland finally bows to the *force majeure* of the new order.

DUNLUCE CASTLE

Dunluce Castle, on the north Antrim coast near Portrush, is the most spectacularly sited castle in Ireland. There was a fortification here from ancient Gaelic times. The present building dates mainly from the sixteenth and seventeenth centuries but parts of the original fourteenth-century structure still survive, and it is on its late medieval role that we start.

At that time, the lands around Dunluce were in the possession of the MacQuillans. They acquired these lands by purchase from the previous owners, the de Mandevilles, in the 1460s. Here was a telling detail. The fourteenth and fifteenth centuries saw a spectacular revival of Gaelic Ireland, as the Hiberno-Norman conquest was first stalled and then, in many places, reversed. Inter-marriage between colonist and Gael and the adoption of Irish forms of dress — and even the Irish language itself — became a source of distress to the king's administration in Dublin. Despite many attempted proscriptions, this 'corruption' of the colony continued apace.

Ulster was lost. The lordship established by de Courcy and won in arms by Hugh de Lacy in 1205 was a distant memory 200 years later. Only Carrickfergus, still impregnable behind its massive walls, held out. The transfer of the lands in north Antrim from the Norman de Mandevilles to the Gaelic MacQuillans was part of this process. And nowhere on the island was the process more complete than in Ulster, which by the end of the Middle Ages was the most purely Gaelic part of Ireland, with no Hiberno-Norman presence whatsoever apart from Carrickfergus.

In the second half of the sixteenth century, the MacQuillans yielded to the MacDonnells, who became masters of Dunluce and of the surrounding lands known as The Route (from the contemporary name for a private army). The MacDonnells had been Lords of the Western Isles but they in turn had felt the weight of the expanding kingdom of Scotland. The Lordship of the Isles was a vestigial survivor of the ancient seaborne kingdom of Dal Riada, which united parts of north-east Ulster and south-west Scotland. But the early Stuart kings of Scotland had ambitions to unite all the territory north of the Tweed to their crown. James III and his son James IV succeeded, having acquired a new and terrifying weapon of war: artillery. Castles were no longer impregnable.

The Lordship of the Isles was suppressed and the title assumed by the King of Scots in 1476. Just to emphasise the point, James IV made an unimpeded royal progress around the isles in the 1490s. The MacDonnells fled south to Ireland, in an ironic inversion of the original colonial enterprise that had created Dal Riada in the fifth century. They settled in the Glens of Antrim, established a formidable lordship there and, as we saw, pushed west into The Route by defeating the MacQuillans in battle. By the late 1500s, their presence in these lands was secure and Dunluce Castle became their principal seat.

The nemesis of the MacQuillans was Sorley Boy MacDonnell. His name is an anglicised version of *Somhairle Buí*, yellow Sorley, this being a reference to his fair hair and not to his courage, which no one doubted. His father had been the last MacDonnell lord of the isles; he re-established his family's fortunes in Ireland. He had been held prisoner in Dublin Castle as a young man, during one of the Dublin administration's attempts to bring what it considered order to Ulster.

The policy of the English government towards Ireland changed after the English Reformation. In 1541, Henry VIII assumed the style and title of King of Ireland, setting aside the medieval Lord of Ireland. In this declaration of kingship, there was an implicit claim to sovereign authority over the whole island. The question was whether this was to be accomplished by persuasion or main force, a policy choice that bedevilled English policy in Ireland for the rest of the sixteenth century, until the Nine Years' War settled the matter for good and all with the final English victory and the submission of Hugh O'Neill at Mellifont.

In the meantime, Sorley Boy was at the centre of the serpentine intrigues that made up the politics of Ulster in the second half of the century. The English attempt at persuasion in Ireland was the policy known as surrender and re-grant, whereby the Gaelic lords would do homage to the monarch (from 1558, Queen Elizabeth I) and in return have their lands re-granted to them under English law and titles. Thus the O'Neills of Tír Eoghan, the most powerful Gaelic family in the island, became earls of Tyrone. Likewise, Sorley Boy made his submission and became Lord of the Route and Constable of Dunluce Castle.

One of the problems with surrender and re-grant was that the succession systems in Irish and English law could hardly have been more different. In Ireland the law of tanistry allowed a chief's successor to be chosen from a wide circle of his relations, whereas English inheritance law was based on primogeniture in the male line. This created obvious problems, not least for the O'Neills.

Conn Bacach (the lame) O'Neill, chief of his ancient clan, had accepted the title of earl of Tyrone under the terms of surrender and regrant. His son Matthew inherited the title on his death and, although probably illegitimate, this succession was deemed to be good in English law. Irish law, however, was quite another matter. The Gaelic laws of succession enabled all of Conn Bacach's sons, at a minimum, to contest the succession. The most ruthless and able of these was Shane O'Neill, the eldest of Conn's sons whose legitimacy was not in question. He had Matthew murdered in 1558 and joined the earldom to the traditional title of The O'Neill which he had made his own.

Shane O'Neill was by far the most powerful Gaelic warlord in Ulster. He faced no internal opposition in his Tyrone heartland and pressed hard on adjacent lordships, including the MacDonnells of Dunluce. English expeditions against him proved futile. Elizabeth could not beat Shane, so she tried to tame him. She invited him to London, where he turned up with a retinue that appeared to Londoners to be both savage and exotic. A compromise was reached in which he was recognised as a captain but not as earl of Tyrone. When O'Neill returned, he proceeded to attack the various Gaelic lordships, including that of Sorley Boy, whom he defeated in 1565 and whose lands he devastated.

Shane did not know when to stop. He overplayed his hand: a series of defeats by the MacSweeneys and O'Donnells of Tír Chonaill (Donegal) in 1567 forced him to flee east. For a reason never properly explained, he sought refuge with Sorley Boy, whom he had humiliated only two years earlier. Why he thought that he might be safe with someone whom he had reduced to tributary status is unclear, but it was a misjudgement that cost him his life. Sorley Boy had him murdered.

As for Sorley Boy himself, he was to feel the weight of English arms in the 1570s and '80s and had to take refuge in Scotland on more than one occasion. But he kept coming back and was finally reconciled to the crown in 1586, four years before his death. He had been one of the great survivors in a turbulent era. His son became the first earl of Antrim, to secure the continuance of the line in English law, although the architecture of the re-built castle at Dunluce contained many typically Scottish features, a reminder of where the MacDonnells of the Glens had hailed from.

11

ROCKFLEET CASTLE

Clew Bay has, it is said, an island for every day of the year. On the outermost and biggest, Clare Island, there is a church whose walls, most unusually for medieval Ireland, contain some frescoes. In the south-east corner, there is a castle belonging to the O'Malleys. In 1530, it was held by Eoghan Dubhdara Ó Máille, chief of a clan of noted sea rovers and traders whose base in Clew Bay was protected by this castle. The O'Malleys controlled the coastal trade, imposed levies and taxes on boats fishing in their waters, and acknowledged the overlordship of the Burkes of Mayo. These were the Gaelicised descendants of the de Burgos, whose coastal lands were protected by a necklace of castles ashore on the mainland. One of these was Rockfleet.

In or around 1530, Eoghan was presented with a daughter who was to become one of the most famous women in Irish history. Gráinne ní Mháille was anglicised as Grace O'Malley, but she is better known to us simply as Granuaile, being the best attempt that English contemporaries could make to pronounce her name.

In no part of the Norman colony had the process of Gaelicisation been more pronounced than in Connacht. It was not the most remote province — that was Ulster — but it was the poorest. There is less good land, whether for tillage or grazing, in Connacht than in the other three provinces. This meant that it was more sparsely populated than the others, simply because it could only support a smaller number of people. That said, the west of Ireland (a very modern imaginative construct) is not an agricultural wasteland. The land is not as lush as the great limestone plains and valleys of Leinster and Munster, but it can and did support something more than a subsistence agriculture. In addition, there was a strong tradition of pre-industrial manufacturing in medieval and early modern Connacht: it was the triple combination of the industrial revolution, the railway revolution and free trade in the first half of the nineteenth century that condemned Connacht — along with many similar regions all over Europe — to relative backwardness, or what was perceived as such.

When Granuaile was born, Galway was a thriving port — the second in Ireland by volume of trade and by far the most important in Connacht. A glance at an atlas will show how well positioned it was for trade with the continental Atlantic seaboard. First and foremost, it imported wine. Salt was also an important commodity as a preservative. Its exports included woollen products manufactured in cottage industries all over the province in a manner typical of the pre-industrial world.

So the province into which she was born was poor but by no means impoverished. Her own family thrived on a mixture of trade and the levying of taxes on foreign vessels fishing in Irish coastal waters. (It is one of the smaller historical mysteries as to why the Irish did not develop their own fishing fleets.) At sixteen years of age, she married Donal O'Flaherty from the famous Connemara family, from whose depredations the citizens of Galway devoutly wished to be delivered. She bore him three children before he was murdered by a rival family and in the meantime she established her reputation as a seafarer.

We know so little about the lives of women in the sixteenth century, indeed in any century prior to the twentieth. So the exploits of Granuaile, even where they are sometime barnacled by legend, are a glimpse into a world of possibility. It was one only open to a high-born woman married to someone of her own rank, as she was. In 1566, she cemented an alliance with *terra firma* by marrying her second husband, Richard

MacWilliam Burke, whose principal fortress was this tower house, Rockfleet Castle. The MacWilliam Burkes were divided by ancient feud into the Lower or northern branch — that into which Granuaile married — and the Upper or southern branch, also known as Clanrickarde. Between them, they were the most powerful family in Connacht.

By the middle of the sixteenth century, the province had passed almost completely out of the control of the English. As with the rest of the island, the second half of century brought a fitful attempt to re-assert the interests of the crown in Connacht, a process that culminated in the so-called Composition of Connacht in 1585.

In the meantime, the English advance meant trouble for families like the MacWilliam Burkes, long used to exercising their local power untrammelled by remote central authority. In 1569, Sir Edward Fitton was appointed first Lord President of the province and he sought to reduce the power of the magnates. He besieged Rockfleet in 1574 without success. Three years later, Granuaile met the English Lord Deputy, Sir Henry Sidney, in Galway, who was well acquainted with her exploits and spoke of her as 'a famous feminine sea captain'. Fitton declared that she 'thinketh herself no small lady'.

She was right: her seaborne power made her reputation and secured her the respect and enmity of the English in equal measure. They referred to her as a pirate queen, although she could not possibly have seen herself in those terms. She was simply applying marine codes and usages of ancient provenance. It was practices such as these that the crown tried to suppress by introducing English law and custom to Connacht in the 1580s. It was easy for them to denounce Granuaile as a pirate, ignoring — when not celebrating — the contemporary piracy on the high seas of Drake and Hawkins.

She was captured for a while and incarcerated in Dublin Castle but returned to north Connacht where her power survived the death of her second husband in 1582. Two years later, the ruthless Sir Richard Bingham became Lord President of Connacht and it was he, by brute force and terror as often as not, who prosecuted the scheme for the Composition of Connacht. He had greater success in the Clanrickarde lands near Galway than in Granuaile's redoubt to the north of the province. None the less, he was a constant threat to her interests and eventually she so wearied of his importunities that she appealed directly to Queen Elizabeth in London, thus leading to one of the most remarkable meetings in Irish history.

In 1593, now in her sixties, she accepted an invitation to visit the queen. She commanded one of her own large galleys, sailing it all the way from Clew Bay to Greenwich. She gave assurances of her good behaviour to the queen — although, not for the first time in her career, she failed to keep them on her return home. Bingham, to his frustration, was instructed to go easy on her. She gave material assistance to the

Gaelic lords of Ulster during the Nine Years' War (1594–1603) in their rebellion against the crown and died in the latter year, the same year as the queen's death. Hers had been a most remarkable life, a bridge between an old world and a new. Her old world was doomed: the English victory in the Nine Years' War spelled death for Gaelic Ireland.

Clew Bay.

12

BLACK TOM BUTLER'S HOUSE

O rmond Manor House is the earliest example we have of an undefended domestic dwelling, a manor house, in early modern Ireland. It was built just outside Carrick-on-Suir in south Tipperary in the mid-1560s close to an earlier tower house. The point about tower houses, like the Burkes' Rockfort Castle in Mayo, was that they were designed for defence. They assumed a steady or intermittent state of war. They are to be seen all over Ireland and they testify to a warlord, marchland society.

Thomas Butler, 10th earl of Ormond, was head of one of the three greatest Hiberno-Norman families established in Ireland. The Butlers of Ormond and Orrery controlled an earldom that ran from Waterford up the valleys of the Barrow, Nore and Suir rivers, and encompassed much of south Leinster and central and south-east Munster. To the north of the earldom lay the lands of the FitzGeralds of Kildare, until the 1530s the greatest family in Ireland. Their fall from grace followed the rebellion of Silken Thomas in 1534, when magnate power met the full force of Henry VIII's centralising ambitions for the first time. To the south and west lay the other branch of the FitzGeralds, the earls of Desmond, the most Gaelicised of all the magnate families, whose domain stretched from the borders of Ormond to the Atlantic.

Tom Butler was a distant cousin of Queen Elizabeth and was educated at court in London, where he made connections that proved useful in later life. He succeeded to the earldom as a minor in the 1540s. Although his mother was one of the FitzGeralds of Desmond, he faced constant border disputes with that family where the two earldoms abutted each other. He was determined to undo gains which the Desmonds had made during his minority. The result was the Battle of Affane in 1565, the last 'private' battle in Irish history between magnate armies. Butler defeated his great rival, Gerald FitzGerald, 15th earl of Desmond, thus precipitating a long and complicated series of events that saw the destruction of the earldom of Desmond in the 1580s following a rebellion that combined resistance both to the religious Reformation and to the centralising power of London.

With the demise of both branches of the FitzGeralds, the Butlers were now the first family of Ireland. None the less, the building of Ormond Manor House represented an act of faith. To be sure, the earldom's principal seat was the mighty castle in Kilkenny to the north, and a cadet branch presided over the tower house at Kilcash on the lower slopes of Slievenamon to the north-west of Carrick. (Kilcash was later to be the inspiration for one of the finest ballad laments in Irish poetry.) Still, first is first and is always impressive. The manor house at Carrick was a declaration in stone that this was a land of peace. Indeed, following Affane both Ormond and Desmond had pledged to the queen that they would henceforth keep the peace. Ormond, shrewd and knowing, maintained his side of the bargain. The unstable and erratic Desmond did not and began the melancholy series of events that encompassed the destruction of his house and lands.

Indeed, Ormond played a notable part in the military response to the Desmond rebellion. Thus, he combined attachment to the crown with religious conviction — he was Protestant — which sat very conveniently with the traditional Butler hostility to Desmond. He embarked on a building programme in Kilkenny: Rothe House (1594) and the Shee Alms House (1582) survive from his time and are among the sights of the modern city.

The significance of the Ormond Manor House has as much to do with its location as its survival. In the inner Pale, and especially in the principal towns of Dublin and Drogheda, English fashions in architecture, dress and fashion were followed. By the middle of the sixteenth century, England itself was full of undefended manor houses, especially in the south. Hatfield Old Palace (not to be confused with the later and current Hatfield House adjacent) dates from 1497, nearly a century before the house at Carrick. Avebury Manor, Garsington and Grimshaw Hall near Birmingham — to name but a few — were all earlier than or near contemporary with the Butler house, and there were dozens of others in a similar category. In France, the utterly spectacular Château de Chambord was finished twenty years before Carrick was started.

Ireland was a marginal place, and what Black Tom Butler's house symbolised was the gradual extension of peaceful, civic life to a marchland that had hitherto been the unstable playground of warlords. Ormond Manor House was before its time: the great era of Irish country houses does not start until the early eighteenth century, with the final Protestant victory that ended the long series of Irish religious–political wars that had dragged on intermittently from the 1530s to the 1690s. Even a structure as big as Portumna Castle, on the Shannon in east Galway, which dates from about 1620 — fifty years after Black Tom's house — still had outer military defences, although the inner core was a manor house. So the house at Carrick, built in the 1560s, is a pioneering structure in a provincial Irish context.

As for Black Tom himself — named for his dark hair rather than his complexion — he proved to be one of the great survivors of an uncertain age. Always close to his cousin the queen, who liked him, he held high military commands in Ireland from her. However, he faced the serial hostility and suspicion of royal governors in Ireland. A pragmatist, he understood the need to make accommodations with older, traditional Irish ways that the New English regarded as barbarous and backward. To the Dublin administration, he was seen as a temporising barrier to what they regarded as progress: the wholesale imposition of English mores and usages in Ireland. He was also suspected, with some justice, of being a closet Catholic, for it seems that he reverted to the old religion prior to his death in 1614. By then, his influence had been diminished following the death of the queen eleven years earlier.

None the less, the Butler interest held on. Four years before Black Tom's death, James Butler was born. He was to be 12th earl and first duke of his line and the effective ruler of Ireland from 1660 to 1688. The family maintained its presence in Kilkenny Castle until

1967, when it gifted the Castle to the state. And in the twentieth century, one of Ireland's finest essayists and controversialists was Hubert Butler, of a cadet branch of the family, whose rediscovery in old age by the reading public was one of the more pleasing features of the 1980s, that otherwise dismal decade.

Rothe House, Kilkenny.

13

THE WALLS OF DERRY

If Ireland is a marginal place in European terms, the Protestants of Ulster sometimes feel like the last, exhausted gasp of the Reformation, and the province itself like the place where the energy gave out. This can be unfair, and it grotesquely misrepresents the self-confident plutocracy of Belfast that dominated eastern Ulster in late Victorian times.

But western Ulster is a different place and always has been. Here, the series of plantations — both private and state sponsored — were more thinly rooted. A greater density of Protestant settlement was achieved in the east of the province, whereas the west was from the beginning at the margin of the plantation exercise — and, generally speaking, the farther one advanced west of the River Bann, the truer this was.

There had been a series of monastic sites on the east bank of the Foyle estuary from ancient times and a small town developed there in late medieval days. This was overrun by Sir Cahir O'Doherty, the Gaelic lord of Inishowen, in 1608. In the previous year, the great Gaelic lords Hugh O'Neill and Hugh O'Donnell, chiefs of their name in Gaelic form and respectively earls of Tyrone and Tyrconnell in English eyes, had fled Ireland after their defeat in the Nine Years' War. This had been the most sustained and concerted resistance to Tudor centralisation anywhere in the British Isles. Considering the amount of blood and treasure expended to defeat the rebellion, the settlement terms were generous and the earls retained their lands. For the moment.

Rather like Black Tom Butler, the earls faced the implacable hostility of the New English administration in Dublin. These men on the ground regarded the treaty that concluded the war as a betrayal of the English and Protestant interest and they harassed Tyrone and Tyrconnell sufficiently to precipitate their departure for the continent in 1607. This was the fabled Flight of the Earls. It was supposed to be temporary, a manoeuvre to acquire Catholic support abroad. It proved permanent, and it left the vast lands controlled by the earls forfeit to the crown. The scene was set for the state-sponsored Plantation of Ulster, a misnomer. Antrim and Down were not part of the scheme, having already been planted by private schemes which were a kind of adjunct to the state scheme.

Derry was settled by members of a number of London craft guilds which formed themselves into the Honourable Irish Society. By royal charter dated 1613, they were granted the lands of what is roughly the modern Co. Derry. They built two early towns, one at Coleraine and the other on the west bank of the Foyle, across the river from the old settlement. It was built on a bluff, rising ground commanding a bend in the estuary and protected by a swamp to the rear, the Bogside. In a nod to its origins, it not only retained the anglicised form of the Gaelic settlement, *Doire*, but prefixed it with London, to give us Londonderry.

The settlers built the walls in five years, completing the protective encirclement of the settlement in 1618. The pattern of the town is roughly diamond-shaped, with defensive bastions at the four corners where the city gates were located. Within the walls, four streets radiated from the central Diamond — the square that echoed the outer pattern of the walls themselves. The plan was rational, rectangular: a little piece of Renaissance urbanity in the far west of Europe. It was one of the last — if not the very last — walled town built anywhere in Europe.

If Ormond Manor House to the south symbolised a land of peace — or at least the aspiration to one — there was no such sentiment in Derry. The city set upon a hill was braced for defence — and it needed to be. It was one of the few urban centres in the province not to fall to the rebels of 1641. But its great symbolic moment came with its successful resistance to the Jacobite siege of 1688. At a time when the forces of James II — the last Catholic king of England and Ireland — were rampant in Ulster, only the citadels of Enniskillen and Londonderry held out.

The story has entered folklore: how the military governor, Lundy, thought the city lost, only to be overthrown and his name ever after used as a synonym for *traitor* in Protestant Ulster; how the apprentice boys of the town slammed shut the gates against the Jacobite forces; how the population, swollen with terrified refugees from the countryside, endured a horrific siege of 105 days, subsisting on vermin and domestic animals until at last a Williamite ship broke the boom that had been thrown across the Foyle by the besiegers and relieved the little town. It had held out against all odds, the unviolated Maiden City of myth.

Derry's Walls became just that: the symbol that furnished the central myth of resistance in the Ulster Protestant imagination. The image of the siege, and the condition of being permanently besieged, has never been far from Protestant consciousness. It has taken root in the belief that the dispossessed natives were ever and always alert to the possibility of undoing the Plantation. In more modern times, it has furnished a powerful symbol for unionism, which sees Irish nationalism precisely in these revanchist terms: an implacable, never-sleeping foe seeking to regain that which was lost.

Towns are like that anyway, often fearing the intentions of those in their hinterland. Dublin feared the Gaelic families of Wicklow for much of the Middle Ages. Galway famously wished to be delivered from the fury of the O'Flahertys, lords of Connemara. In Derry, that was a sustainable position for as long as the little town was solidly Protestant. But the industrial revolution in the nineteenth century brought an influx of people from the surrounding countryside, and especially from Catholic Donegal. Before the end of the century, the city had a Catholic majority and had spread well beyond the walls.

None the less, the local Protestant hegemony was maintained for most of the twentieth century by an ingenious and shameless succession of electoral boundary changes and gerrymandering. Partition in 1921 helped this, although the border ran close to the city. The devolved government in Belfast — solidly Unionist and designed to be so — winked at the antics in the west, if at times finding them a bit Baroque. It was hardly surprising that when the boil eventually burst in 1969 and the Troubles began, they began in Derry. The Maiden City had effectively fallen at last.

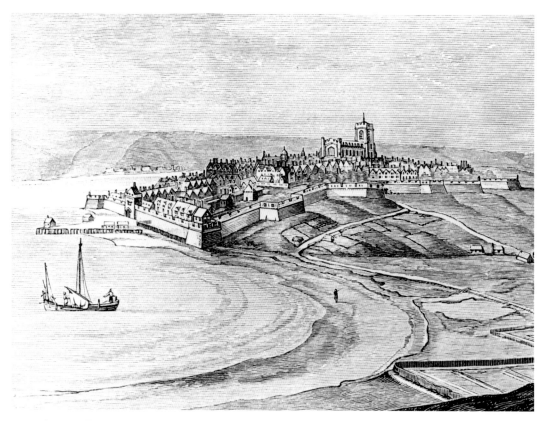

An early view of the walled town of Derry.

ST MARY'S COLLEGIATE CHURCH, YOUGHAL

The small town of Youghal stands at the mouth of the Blackwater, one of the principal rivers of south Munster. There was a monastic settlement here in early Christian times and there is evidence of a Viking presence in the eighth and ninth centuries. But the town does not really acquire the sinews of urbanity until the early thirteenth century, when the Normans secured its first charter.

The town was devastated in 1579 during the great Desmond rebellion, but it recovered quickly after the end of hostilities. It passed into the ownership of Sir Walter Raleigh until 1602, when, strapped for cash, he sold it to Richard Boyle for a knockdown price.

Boyle was the classic man on the make. A yeoman's son from Kent, he studied at Cambridge and the Middle Temple in London. He arrived in Ireland in 1588 and, using forged letters of introduction, managed to insinuate his way into government circles. He was rewarded by securing the appointment of deputy escheator, which meant that he had responsibility for the disposal and administration of lands forfeit to the crown. This was a position well suited to his talent for corruption and peculation. As a result, he drew the enmity of a number of influential figures in government and even spent some time in prison in the early 1590s.

In 1595, he married a well-connected heiress who brought him a modest fortune, although this was much diminished by the depredations of the Nine Years' war in Munster. Once again, his enemies brought charges against him but he successfully defended himself in London, where he enjoyed the queen's protection. She liked his dash and seemed prepared to wink at his malfeasance. His wife died in childbirth in 1599 (the child also died) and Boyle remarried four years later. His second wife — and mother of his many children — was the daughter of an Irish privy councillor. Boyle was now a man of substance, having secured both financial fortune and social position.

From here, his rise was irresistible. He was knighted on his wedding day in 1603, appointed privy councillor for Munster in 1606, for Ireland in 1613, elected an Irish MP in 1614, titled as Lord Youghal in 1616 and finally established as 1st earl of Cork in 1620. By now, he had become the richest man in Ireland. He had been able to pay £4,000 to Sir George Villiers, the royal favourite and soon to be the duke of Buckingham, to secure his earldom. By the late 1620s, he was able to lend King Charles I the enormous sum of £15,000 at short notice.

The great earl of Cork, as he became known, was full of energy. He was responsible for establishing or greatly improving many towns, including Clonakilty, Charleville, Midleton and Doneraile. In Youghal, he built the Widows' Alms Houses (1602) and established himself in a splendid new house, The College, beside the Collegiate church. This he also restored and improved — although not to the extent that he had promised — and in the south transept he placed a splendid tomb to commemorate himself and his family (illustrated, p. 49). It is the principal attraction of the church today. Little of the fabric of St Mary's survives from the great earl's time, having been the victim of yet another insensitive Victorian 'restoration'.

He was also an early industrialist and established many ironworks, being one of a number of New English adventurers to do likewise. His ironworks required charcoal, which he supplied by felling hundreds of acres of trees. It was little wonder that the Gaelic poet who lamented the fall of the Butler house at Kilcash wrote,

Cad a dhéanfaimid feasta gan adhmad? / Tá deireadh na gcoillte ar lár

Or in Frank O'Connor's translation (with Yeats's hand very visible)

What shall we do for timber? / The last of the woods is down

In his pomp, Cork lived like a medieval magnate, semi-autonomous in his own domain. It was a bilingual world, and while the earl spoke no Irish his four-year-old son did and acted as translator for his father. He adopted Irish usages, such as fostering his children among reliable tenants (thus presumably accounting for his little boy's bilingualism) and having Irish-speaking Catholics both as servants and tenants.

He brooked no opposition. In 1627, an ironmaster with whom he was in dispute was arrested in Youghal despite carrying a safe passage from the king. The earl ignored this and made the man amenable to his own palatine justice. He was not one to be crossed and he resented any intrusion into his personal realm. Central authority was far away and as far as the earl was concerned that was the best place for it.

This brought him into conflict with Sir Thomas Wentworth, appointed lord deputy of Ireland in 1632. A centraliser determined to assert royal prerogatives in all corners of Ireland, Wentworth managed to alienate every important interest group in the country. He might have expected problems with the Old English (the descendants of the medieval Hiberno-Normans) and the remaining Gaelic families on account of their shared Catholicism. But his natural allies should have been New English Protestants like the earl of Cork. His attempts to foist the high church principles of the king and archbishop Laud of Canterbury on the Church of Ireland — where low church, Puritan attitudes were entrenched — did not help.

It got personal. The earl, who was much devoted to funerary monuments for himself and his family, had one erected in Christ Church cathedral in Dublin. Wentworth thought it vulgar and ostentatious and insensitively situated. He forced the earl to remove it to another part of the church. Even worse was the question of the impropriations: the sequestering of church lands and assets by rich laymen. Wentworth was determined to reverse this and to recover these assets for the crown. The earl of Cork was by no means the only offender but he was singled out by Wentworth as an over-mighty subject and exactly the sort of slippery provincial operator whose stratagems offended against everything that Wentworth aspired to: rational and uniform administration in the king's name. He had the earl arraigned before the Court of Castle Chamber (the Irish equivalent of Star Chamber). Eventually, the two met face-to-face and agreed a fine of £30,000 in full settlement, subsequently halved. Wentworth had made himself a dangerous enemy.

Just how dangerous became clear in 1640 when Charles I and the English parliament were on the collision course that led to the English civil war and the execution of the king. The Irish parliament, in which the earl's faction was a significant element, adopted a remonstrance against Wentworth which they sent to the London parliament. That body feared that the lord deputy was raising an Irish Catholic army to bring over to England, and had Wentworth recalled. The earl travelled to London and gave evidence against Wentworth, who was impeached, tried, convicted and executed.

The earl of Cork died in 1643 aged 77. He left a distinguished line. His eldest surviving son, also Richard (1612–98), became 2nd earl of Cork, 1st earl of Burlington in the English peerage and lord high treasurer of Ireland from 1660 until 1695. His younger son, Roger Boyle (1621–79), became Lord Broghill and later 1st earl of Orrery. As Broghill, he was one of the more ferocious Cromwellian commanders. The fourth son, Francis Boyle (1623–99), became the 1st Viscount Shannon: his grandson Henry, earl of Shannon, was speaker of the Irish House of Commons from 1733 to 1753. The youngest son of the great earl, Robert (1627–91), made the most lasting contribution to the world. Often spoken of as the father of English chemistry, he enunciated the law that bears his name, a formula known to generations of schoolchildren, although happily forgotten by adults.

MILLMOUNT, DROGHEDA

H ere, we are only a few kilometres east of Slane Priory (chapter 1) near the
mouth of the Boyne. Drogheda, yet another town of Norman
foundation, stands at the tidal reach of the river. The Boyne Valley,
running inland to the west, was one of the most continuously settled
areas in the island since deep antiquity. It has been speculated that the Millmount,
standing proud on the south shore of the river, may have been a Neolithic burial cairn
like Newgrange nearby. There seems little means of proving this hypothesis; at any rate,
the site assumed the classic appearance of a Norman motte.

A motte is a circular mound, an earthwork. It usually accommodated a fortress on top, called a bailey. Motte and bailey fortifications had been developed in France in early medieval times and were deployed by the Normans in the various territories they occupied, including Ireland. In the age before artillery, they represented formidable defensive positions.

The Millmount was certainly a Norman motte, whether of original construction or adapted from a more ancient structure we don't know. Its purpose was to protect the bridge over the Boyne in the little town below. By the late Middle Ages, Drogheda had grown into one of the most important towns in the east of Ireland. It was the occasional site of the peripatetic Irish parliament (which did not settle permanently in Dublin until the early seventeenth century).

It was at a parliament meeting in Drogheda in 1494 that Poynings' Law was enacted, one of the great examples in Irish history of the law of unintended consequences. Its purpose was to ensure that no Irish parliament could meet, nor could any bills be introduced, without the permission of the English king. It was designed for a contemporary purpose: to ensure that no pretender to the English throne (in an age of dynastic uncertainty) could be crowned in an Irish parliament, as had happened with the hapless Lambert Simnel a few years earlier. Had Poynings realised that this piece of contingent legislation would have been a constitutional *cause célèbre* nearly three hundred years later, no one would have been more surprised than he.

By the 1640s, Drogheda was one of the more important walled towns of the Pale and a centre of Old English influence. It was therefore cast into the maelstrom of events that engulfed the British Isles in that decade. The rebellion against the arbitrary rule of Charles I and his ministers began in Scotland in 1638. Within three years, the Scots had defeated the king's army and had devastated the north of England. Charles was forced to recall parliament to vote supplies, thus ending eleven years of personal rule. Parliament wanted constitutional and religious concessions in return — it was much more Puritan in temper than the royal government — and the result was the two English civil wars and the execution of the king in 1649.

In 1641, there was a rising of Ulster Catholics against the new Protestant settlers introduced by the Plantation of Ulster. At first, it was centred on a number of Ulster Gaelic lords who wished to seize Dublin Castle, take control of the Irish administration (but in the king's name) and undo the Plantation. The plot was betrayed and failed, but a rising broke out in Ulster and quickly ran out of the control of the leaders. There were massacres. The numbers were later exaggerated for propaganda purposes but the reality was grim enough without exaggeration: perhaps a quarter of the settler population was put to the sword, an atrocity that burned itself indelibly into the Ulster Protestant folk memory.

The rebellion spread south and faced the Old English with a dilemma. They made an historic compromise and for the first time ever made common cause with their fellow Catholics of Gaelic origin, reckoning that a rebellion in the king's name would be rewarded with better terms if Charles won in England than they could hope for from parliament. The Confederation of Kilkenny was the result, but the tensions between Gael and Old English were never far below the surface. As to their hopes, the king did not win in England. In August 1649, the newly-triumphant parliament sent their best general to Ireland to settle matters there.

Oliver Cromwell made it clear from the start that he intended to avenge the Ulster massacres of 1641. He besieged Drogheda, spending two days in a carefully calculated artillery barrage on the town walls. He drove most of the defenders to the bastion of the Millmount, where the garrison was slaughtered without quarter: the commander, Sir Arthur Aston, was beaten to death with his own wooden leg. Then the troops were turned loose on the town for two days. Cromwell saw the massacre at Drogheda as exemplary and condign revenge for 1641, as well as a means of terrifying other towns into meek submission. Having repeated the dose at Wexford a few weeks later, he quickly proceeded to do what no English commander had managed in almost five hundred years: the total subjection of Ireland to an English ruler. But the price paid was heavy. Cromwell's name was burned into Irish Catholic collective memory as thoroughly as the Ulster killings of 1641 were in Protestant memory. The English victory had been born of a massacre. It was an ill omen.

The final conquest of the island was accompanied by famine and plague. There were other exemplary massacres as well, although nothing on the theatrical scale of Drogheda. The country was devastated, a classic case of making a desert and calling it peace. There followed an Act of Settlement which dispossessed nearly all Catholic landowners in Leinster and Munster and removed them to smaller holdings in Connacht, west of the Shannon. Cromwell was completely indifferent and insensitive to the ancient division between Gael and Old English. To him, Catholics were an undifferentiated mass. If later Irish nationalism was confessional in tone, it took its lead from Cromwell.

Eleven million acres were confiscated. On these lands were settled a mixture of soldiers from the New Model Army and people who had financed its campaigns. Twenty years earlier, over 80 per cent of land in the expropriated provinces had been in Catholic hands. Now, in theory at least, not one remained. The descendants of the new landowning class would in time mutate into the Protestant Ascendancy of the eighteenth century. In the meantime, England wearied of Cromwell's personal rule. Two years after his death, Charles II, son of the executed king, came home from his travels.

An aerial view of Drogheda.

ROYAL HOSPITAL

The new king's man in Ireland was James Butler, that grandson of Black Tom Butler who had been born in 1610 (see chapter 12). He served Charles II as he had once served Charles I and the Restoration saw him raised to a dukedom as 1st duke of Ormond.

The duke faced a delicate task. The Restoration of the monarchy had raised hopes among the Catholic dispossessed that the Cromwellian land settlement would be overturned or at least gravely weakened. It soon became clear that neither Ormond nor the king felt willing or able to satisfy these hopes. The new regime was neither strong enough nor secure enough to satisfy such demands. The pattern of land ownership established by Cromwell was to endure until the Land Acts of the late nineteenth and early twentieth centuries, which broke up the estates and established the former tenants as proprietors.

Ormond's task in Ireland generally was to maintain the delicate equilibrium of the new regime, in short to eschew adventures. In Dublin, however, his presence was transformative. It is no accident that Maurice Craig begins his acclaimed account of the city in its classical age with the arrival of the duke, stepping 'out of his pinnace on to the sands of Dublin Bay'. It was 27 July 1662 and, in Craig's lapidary summary, 'the Middle Ages were at last at an end'.

Dublin did indeed begin to acquire some of the sinews of the modern city. From the early seventeenth century, it had become the sole seat of the Irish parliament. The Restoration also brought the gradual return of economic growth. The city began to expand again, with notable suburban development on the north bank of the Liffey and to the west of the walls towards Kilmainham. A city that had only ever had one bridge acquired four more between 1670 and 1683. Three of these bridges still exist, although all have been reconstructed over time.

Perhaps the most enduring legacy bequeathed the city by the Duke of Ormond is the Phoenix Park. On his arrival in 1662, he took up residence in the Phoenix Manor, which stood on the site of the modern Magazine Fort. He acquired 2,000 acres around the Manor as a viceregal deer park. One of the previous owners from whom he bought the land was Sir Maurice Eustace, the speaker of the Irish House of Commons, whose name lives on in a street in Temple Bar. The duke stocked the park with deer, whose descendants are still to be seen there today.

Another notable Ormond legacy is St Stephen's Green. This had existed from medieval times as a pasture area for cattle and horses in the distant south-east reaches of the small town. By 1664, when its 27 acres were denominated by the Dublin Corporation as a public leisure area, it was still distant from the city centre. Building lots were sold to enclose the green and were gradually developed for town houses. There was a problem, however. The route linking Trinity College and the Green was deemed to be 'so foule and out of repair that persons cannot pass to the said Green for the benefit of the walks therein'. Something had to be done and in 1671 the Corporation set about the improvements that in time led to the development of Grafton Street.

The 1680s brought a building boom to Dublin. Churches were built or rebuilt. Francis Place's panoramic drawing of the city in 1698 shows seventeen church towers and spires, giving the cityscape a vertical definition that it had previously lacked. The Liberties became increasingly populated and densely housed, as the area also became the centre of Huguenot life in the city. Like many talented exiles, they contributed to their host societies in a manner out of all proportion to their numbers. They were skilled craftsmen, especially talented at textile weaving and silk production. Their industry encouraged the development of these trades in Dublin; the name Weaver Street in the modern Liberties is a reminder of their presence.

Every age of construction requires a stand-out building, one that defines the era. Caroline Dublin was no exception. Most of the 1680s was consumed in the construction of the greatest civic building in the seventeenth-century city, and the first one that was unambiguously post-Renaissance in design. The Royal Hospital at Kilmainham was built as a residence for homeless ex-soldiers on the express instructions of the duke. The model — intellectual if not architectural — was Les Invalides in Paris. The foundation stone was laid by the duke himself in 1680 and the building was completed in 1687, making it older by a few years than Chelsea Hospital in London. The first veterans were admitted in 1684. The distinctive tower is a slightly later addition, dating from 1701. The architect of this splendid building was Sir William Robinson, the surveyor-general of Ireland. (He was also the designer of Marsh's Library, beside St Patrick's cathedral, and had a hand in many other improvements including those at Dublin Castle.) It occupies an elevated site in what was then a western suburb, on lands formerly held by the Order of Knight Hospitallers of St John of Jerusalem, standing to the south of the river across from the Phoenix Park on the far bank.

The arcaded inner quadrangle has a distinctly Italian feel to it and its cool Renaissance classicism is in sharp contrast to the Baroque exuberance of the chapel. It fulfilled its original function, accommodating up to 300 veterans, until 1927. Williamite troops wounded at the battle of Aughrim in 1691 stayed here and crown troops were billeted at the Hospital during the 1916 rising.

THE GARDINER
ESTATE

O f the new bridges built in Restoration Dublin, the most important was the one on the site of the modern Capel Street bridge. For all of its history, the city's centre of gravity gradually moved from its medieval core around Christ Church eastward towards the bay. Western overspill beyond the walls was suburban rather than urban. Capel Street bridge was originally known as Essex bridge, named for Arthur Capel, earl of Essex, who was lord lieutenant of Ireland from

1672 to 1677, Ormond having been withdrawn for a few years. In 1875 it was renamed for Henry Grattan, the eighteenth-century parliamentarian, but everyone calls it Capel Street bridge.

The new bridge was built between 1676 and 1678. The ubiquitous Sir William Robinson had a hand in its design. It created a new north–south axis from the Castle and made the development of the northern suburbs beyond a tempting prospect. This is exactly what happened in the great eighteenth-century building boom, with the earliest fashionable Georgian developments located north of the river. For the first time, the city was going to occupy both sides of the Liffey.

The bridge begged a street on the far side and it was duly developed by Sir Humphrey Jervis and tactfully named for the lord lieutenant, Jervis contenting himself with the name of a parallel side street. It led towards Drumcondra Lane, the traditional exit route from the city to the north. But it also led to lands that had originally been part of the Cistercian Abbey of St Mary, which had been suppressed at the time of the dissolution of the monasteries. These passed through various secular hands until they were bought by Luke Gardiner MP, the vice-treasurer of Ireland, in 1721.

In the forty years since Capel Street bridge was built, Ireland had finally settled the question of who constituted the ruling class. When Charles II died in 1685, he was succeeded by his brother James II, a Catholic, who unwisely attempted a Catholic restoration. He was ousted from the English throne when his wife gave birth to a healthy son in 1688 — the same year that the duke of Ormond died — in a *coup d'état* ever after dignified as the Glorious Revolution. He tried haplessly to restore his fortunes in Ireland, but defeats at the Boyne and Aughrim put the Protestant victory beyond any further dispute. The long age of the Ascendancy had begun.

Luke Gardiner was a banker whose personal background was obscure. He married into the aristocratic Mountjoy family. It was he who oversaw the early development of the Gardiner estate in the north-east of the city during the first half of the eighteenth century. His grandson, also Luke, Lord Mountjoy (1745–98: he was killed at the Battle of New Ross leading crown troops against the Wexford rebels), was the principal figure in the second half.

Luke Gardiner the Elder bought and developed all of what is now the area east of Capel Street as far as O'Connell Street and Parnell Square. He first developed the area at the northern end of Capel Street. Bolton Street dates from 1720 but the real triumph was Henrietta Street, dating from a few years later (illustrated, p. 57). Here, on lands originally belonging to the Cistercians, Gardiner built enormous town houses, including one for himself at number 10, vastly more spacious than anything else put up in the

Georgian era. The hallways alone are huge, bigger than the total floor area of many modern suburban houses. One of the first residents was Hugh Boulter, archbishop of Armagh, a key political and social figure of the day. Fashion — not least clerical fashion — followed him. Before long, Henrietta Street was known colloquially as Primate's Hill. It helped to establish the north-east suburbs of the city as the centre of early fashionable life. The drift of the beau monde to the south side did not start in earnest until the second half of the century.

This Luke Gardiner was also responsible for the development of Gardiner's Mall, later to mutate into Sackville Street and later again to O'Connell Street. When Gardiner acquired it in 1714, it was known as Drogheda Street (or Lane). This was named for Henry Moore, earl of Drogheda, who is commemorated in Henry Street, Moore Street, Earl Street and Of Lane, all of which have survived. Gardiner widened it by knocking down most of the existing properties — it was an unsentimental business, not encumbered by modern concepts of planning and conservation — and creating a central mall that ran from what is now Parnell Street to the modern Spire. This central area was named Gardiner's Mall, the two parallel sides Sackville Street — named for Lionel Sackville, Duke of Dorset, lord lieutenant in the 1730s. The unwidened lower end retained the name Drogheda Street (thus giving the earl a full house, for the moment at least) until the extension of Sackville Street to the river in the 1780s. Meanwhile the lord lieutenant was further immortalised in Dorset Street, which was developed (but not by Gardiner) along the line of the old Drumcondra Lane.

Shortly before his death, Luke Gardiner the Elder began the development of Rutland Square (now Parnell Square) which in time became a major centre of fashion, never more so than when Lord Charlemont built his town house in Portland stone — to distinguish it from the mere brick of the mansions adjacent — in the 1760s. It is now the Hugh Lane Gallery.

At the corner of Rutland Square nearest the top of Sackville Street, Bartholomew Mosse acquired four acres of land in 1748. Mosse was the proprietor of the Lying-In Hospital, the first dedicated maternity hospital in the world, which he had founded in George's Lane (now South Great George's Street) three years earlier. On this site he planned to build a larger maternity hospital and he engaged Richard Cassels, a Huguenot from Hesse in Germany who had inherited the practice of Edward Lovett Pearce and established himself as the leading Dublin architect of the 1730s and 1740s. Cassels did not live to see his design realised but it was completed by his pupil John Ensor. The Roto — a Dublin landmark ever since — opened on 8 December 1757.

The legacy of three generations of the Gardiner family was absolutely transformative.

It was not just that they developed Dublin to the east of the medieval core: they started the process whereby the mental centre of the city moved east with them. The broad axis of Sackville Street, leading to the bridge and later to connect with the new D'Olier and Westmoreland Streets, combined with the earl of Leinster's decision in 1745 to build his town house south of the river — where fashion followed him, never to return north — created the basic geography of the modern city.

In a sense, the Gardiners were too successful. In developing the north side, they must have thought that its rising ground would have been ideal for their wealthy clientele, for wealth has always coveted an eminence. Instead, in yet another demonstration of the law of unintended consequences, they opened up an avenue to the south. The area around Leinster House, now the most fashionable part of the city, was gradually being developed in the early eighteenth century but not at all as intensively as the Gardiner estate on the north side. The earl of Leinster's move was decisive, although there were problems in the area that did not afflict the north side. Not the least of these was marshy ground and the danger of flooding from the river. The low-lying south side suffered severe flooding in 1735, 1746, 1761 and 1764. In 1792, a breach in the retaining wall of Sir John Rogerson's Quay allowed a party of sportsmen to sail a boat on the flood waters that delivered them to the back garden of a house in Merrion Square! No matter: fashion had moved south and, floods or no floods, there it stayed.

PRINTING HOUSE, TCD

The printing press came late to Ireland. The European invention of printing by moveable type is usually credited to Johannes Gutenberg of Mainz and dated to 1454. It was a revolutionary development. Printing spread like a bush fire in the European core but was slower to take root at the periphery. The first printed books in Paris and Venice appeared in 1470. Ten years later, more than 100 towns had printing presses, the most easterly being Cracow, the most southerly Naples. By 1500, it is estimated that there were already 70 million volumes in circulation — the so-called incunabula — and the number of towns with presses was 236. In the course of the sixteenth century, more than 130,000 new books were published in France, Germany, Italy, England and the Netherlands.

The earliest tentative evidence of book printing in Ireland dates to the mid-sixteenth century. There was no Irish-language translation of the Bible available until 1603. The contrast with Wales is instructive: the earliest Welsh translation of the Book of Common Prayer dates from 1567, although Wales did not have its own press until 1718. In part, both the Irish and Welsh experiences reflected the early centralisation of printing in London, a process for which there was no parallel in the fissiparous German lands. The fonts required to print in Irish did not exist and had to be specially cut. Even then, the 1603 translation was of the New Testament only. A translation of the Old Testament, based on the Authorised Version, did not appear until 1682. Nor was the situation of printing in English much better, so that Maurice Craig claims that anything printed in Ireland before 1700 — that is to say, more than 200 years after printing is firmly established in the continental core — can be regarded as rare.

And yet, within a generation, Dublin was being spoken of as a great European city. One visitor in the 1730s reckoned that only London, Paris, Rome and Amsterdam had bigger populations. This is surely an exaggeration: Barcelona, Madrid, Naples, Vienna and Stockholm were almost certainly bigger. None the less, even an error of this kind indicates the speed with which Dublin, hitherto the deeply undistinguished capital of a remote peripheral place, was catching up. Part of that process was its ability to attract professional artists and craftsmen from the continent.

Richard Cassels (or Castle as he is sometimes styled) was born in Hesse-Kassel in Germany around 1690. An army engineer by profession, his early interest in fortifications mutated into a talent for architecture. By the age of thirty-five, he was in England, from where he was invited by Sir Gustavus Hume, a Fermanagh country gentleman, to design him the house that became Castle Hume. He became an employee of Edward Lovett Pearce, who was then working on his iconic Parliament House. When Pearce died young, Cassels inherited his architectural practice and for the next twenty years until his death in 1751 he was the leading member of his profession in the city and probably in the country.

The Printing House in Trinity College Dublin is one of his early efforts, a simple Doric structure which housed the college's printing press. It still stands, the oldest surviving printing house in Ireland.

The printing press was the information superhighway of the pre-electronic age. As in so many other matters, Ireland may have been a latecomer to the feast but in the course of the eighteenth century, the country moves decisively from marginal irrelevance in European terms to something approaching modernity. Of course, in our terms, this is still a pre-modern age: the industrial and French revolutions are still in the future. That is hardly the point: to contemporaries, Ireland appeared ever more connected to that greater continental culture — whose four corners might roughly be said to embrace the area bounded by London, Stockholm, Budapest, Naples and Lisbon.

This was not an even process and was obviously more marked at the elite than at the popular level. The illiterate peasantry did not commission country houses or go on the Grand Tour. But neither did the illiterate peasantry anywhere, and the continent swarmed with them.

Perhaps the key development in eighteenth-century Ireland is its accelerating urbanisation, creating the sinews of commerce, exchange and a public sphere. In this process, printing was central. Irish printers were able to reprint books without the permission of the rights owners, even though these books enjoyed copyright protection in the larger island under the so-called Statute of Anne of 1710, the world's first copyright act. These books could then be sold in Ireland, and the Irish printers also developed a brisk trade for their wares in North America. However, the monopolist influence of the London printers was sufficient to keep Irish editions out of England, the one market that the Irish really desired. Interestingly, the London trade was less successful in baulking the Scots, whose subsequent influence on British publishing can be traced to this failure.

It was not just books and it was not just Dublin. The Belfast *News Letter* is the oldest continuously published newspaper in the British Isles. It dates from 1737. The *Freeman's Journal*, from the nineteenth century the mouthpiece of the Irish nationalist movement, was first published in 1763. The *Munster Journal*, reckoned to be the first newspaper established in the province, dates from the same period and was succeeded by the *Limerick Journal* in the 1780s. The *Limerick Chronicle* followed shortly thereafter. These, and similar publishing ventures in other provincial centres, were central to the formation of a new public opinion, and anticipated both the explosion of provincial papers in the next century and the arrival of the national press once the railway system furnished the means of countrywide distribution.

The whole process was kick-started in the first half of the eighteenth century, as Ireland began to enjoy the benefits of the long peace that followed the decisive Protestant victory in the Williamite wars. Cassels' chaste and dignified Printing House stands as a symbol of this developing urbanity and the burgeoning public sphere that carried all of

Ireland towards modernity. Ironically, the process of deeper engagement with mainland Europe was amplified by the necessity of training Catholic clergy in the various continental Irish colleges because of the penal laws, thus producing a Catholic high command that was at least as sophisticated as — and certainly more polyglot than — the clergy of the Established Church.

A page from the Gutenberg Bible (above) and an early European printing press.

NEWTOWN PERY

I rish Georgian architecture is recognisably a variation on what was the prevailing international style in the second half of the eighteenth century. One can observe common patterns, as well as marked differences of detail and materials, in cities as far apart as London, Bath, Edinburgh and Dublin. But all share a common architectural grammar, with variations in theme and detail dictated as much by the availability of local materials as anything else.

In Bath local honey-coloured stone, reminiscent of that in the Seine valley across the Channel, dominates. In Edinburgh, it is the massive granite facades of the New Town that impose themselves upon the eye; combined with Auld Reekie's unforgiving climate, they also make these massive houses impossible to heat. In Ireland, Georgian facades are clothed in brick, the island being well provided in brickworks. The warm, russet-brown bricks so characteristic of Irish Georgian house-fronts, combined with their chaste rectilinear design, give the houses their peculiar blend of monumentality and domesticity.

When we think of Irish Georgian, we usually think of Dublin. But Dublin is only part of the story, for this local interpretation of the prevailing international style reached into many corners of the island. In urban terms, nowhere is this better observed than in Limerick.

Like so many Irish cities, Limerick was of Viking foundation, was later occupied by the kings of Thomond and later again by the Normans. Its urban charter dates from 1197. It is in three parts. The heart of the historic town is King's Island, formed by the broad sweep of the Shannon to the west and a small channel, known as the Abbey river, which girdles the island to the east and then rejoins the main river. This historic core was called English town. To the south-east, and across the Abbey river, was Irish town, originally a suburb but later the location for some fine streets, many wider than the cramped and twisted thoroughfares of English town.

The area to the west of Irish town, between it and the Shannon, was open country in the mid-eighteenth century. It is now the centre of the modern city. This is due to the enterprise of the man who owned this land. He was Edmund Sexton Pery MP (1719–1806), who was Speaker of the Irish parliament from 1771 to 1785. In 1765, he asked Davis Ducart to plan a new town on this land. Ducart was an architect from Sardinia — Daviso du Arcort in the pre-anglicised version — who had established himself as a skilful practitioner of the Palladian style in Ireland. In Limerick, he designed the impressive courthouse in Irish town (1769).

Just as Edinburgh New Town was built adjacent to but separate from the historic core of the city, so it was in Limerick. Two things are striking about it. Ducart copied the prevailing Dublin Georgian style for his Limerick buildings and he laid the new town out on a rational rectangular grid plan, one of the very few examples of this kind of street pattern in Ireland. Instead of the medieval jumble of English town, this was a new kind of urbanity: the geometry of the Enlightenment. The whole area was named for its prime mover: Newtown Pery.

Its effect on contemporary sensibility can be measured from Fitzgerald and McGregor's *History, Topography and Antiquities of the County and City of Limerick*, published in 1827 when there were still people alive who could remember Newtown Pery as green fields. They note that an earlier writer of 1775 had reckoned 3,859 houses and 27 streets in the city. Now they estimated 'near seventy streets beside innumerable lanes' and 8,268 houses. The population had grown from an estimate of fewer than 30,000 in 1775 to 66,042 in the census of 1821 (admittedly not as reliable statistically as later censuses).

They rhapsodised this urban novelty.

> The ground on which the New Town is built is rather elevated, and the soil in general gravelly and dry. The streets are spacious, cut each other at right angles, and are occupied by elegant houses and merchants' stores constructed of brick and limestone, for which the neighbouring district supplies the finest materials. A more superb city-view can hardly be presented to the eye than the range of buildings from the New Bridge to the Crescent, a distance little short of an English mile... Shops tastefully laid out and richly furnished line these streets, while others diverge to right and left, which are chiefly occupied by the residences of the gentry.

For novelty it was, and even today it contrasts sharply with the general run of Irish streetscapes, characterised as they are more by irregularity and random individuality than by coherence. By contrast Newtown Pery, in the finest expression of Enlightenment principles, is all coherence and unity of purpose. Symbolically, Fitzgerald and McGregor note that 'at night the streets of the New Town are splendidly lighted with gas, while those of the English Town are left with unaccountable negligence in total darkness, except where the brilliancy of some public house illumines the gloomy scene'.

The later history of Limerick has not always been happy, although it was a vigorous centre of trade and commerce in the nineteenth century. In more recent times, it has had the worst press of any Irish town and has a wretched reputation for gangland violence and drug-related crime. But Newtown Pery still stands as a symbol of rational possibility in brick and stone, one of the most impressive urban landscapes in Ireland.

Irish history is often imagined in terms of the nationalist imperative: the recovery of 'our' country from the strangers who invaded it long ago. But strangers, invaders and immigrants are the very currency of a dynamic country, and especially of port cities. Newtown Pery is not really Irish in the sense that it is not native — if by native we mean Gaelic, Catholic and rural, which all too often we were inclined to do — but it is decisively Irish in another sense. It was built in an Irish manner, an unmistakable variation upon an international theme, at the bidding of a wealthy local grandee. If you were dropped blindfold into Newtown Pery (or Merrion Square) you could not mistake them for anywhere else in the world. There are many ways of being Irish.

CASTLETOWN FOLLY

L ike all pre-modern societies, eighteenth-century Ireland was profoundly unequal. It was an aristocratic society with a colonial settler elite at the top. Most of these were parvenus, beneficiaries of the Cromwellian land settlements, although the position was not quite as stark as that. There was also a surprising degree of social mobility, as is best seen in the case of William Conolly (1662–1729), the son of a minor Catholic landlord and innkeeper from Co. Donegal who had conformed to the Church of Ireland. Through canny land dealing in the confiscations that followed the Williamite war, Conolly made his fortune. He married into a distinguished Williamite family, then entered the Irish parliament, where he demonstrated a talent for political intrigue and manoeuvre that brought him to eminence as Speaker of the Irish House of Commons. He was also the richest commoner in Ireland, rich enough to commission and have built Castletown, the finest classical country house in Ireland, to a design modelled on the Palazzo Farnese in Rome (illustrated, p. 71).

Conolly had risen from the ranks. In the pre-industrial age, 'people of the middling sort' were not a significant element of society. In the towns, they comprised a small professional and commercial class; in the countryside, a rural middle class of substantial tenants — many of them former Catholic landowners reduced to their new status by the Cromwellian confiscations. The vast majority of the population were rural peasants, either sub-tenants or landless labourers. Only in parts of Ulster was there a rural yeoman class, whose farming incomes were supplemented by the domestic production of linen.

The new masters of Ireland were the victors in the Williamite war, the new Anglican elite. The Jacobite attempt to reverse the Cromwellian land settlement had been an existential threat to their interests and it was they — through legislation enacted in the Irish parliament, which they dominated — who dishonoured the relatively generous terms of the Treaty of Limerick that had ended the war. Here was a reprise of the Dublin administration's hounding of the Ulster earls after the end of the Nine Years' War: the people on the ground took a much tougher line with the vanquished than the distant government in London.

From the 1690s to the 1720s, a series of penal laws were enacted with the intention of copper-fastening the social and economic hegemony of this new Anglican elite. Their purpose was not conversion, rather the neutering of Catholics (and to a lesser degree Dissenters) in the public sphere. Most Catholic clergy were banished; Catholics could not educate their children abroad; they could not purchase land or hold leases for more than 31 years; they could not practise law; if a Catholic landowner died, partible inheritance was forced on his sons, unless one conformed, in which case he alone inherited. The whole point was to emasculate what was left of the Catholic landowning class. In an age in which confessional allegiance mattered politically, such legal proscriptions against minorities were not unusual in Europe. What was unusual in the Irish context was their deployment against the majority.

While the penal laws were not rigorously enforced, they were evidence of a society, outwardly at peace, where confessional and ethnic tensions were close to the surface. And while the musculature of the Catholic church survived the penal laws very well — all dioceses had resident bishops in place by 1745 — they were a source of tension and anxiety for old Catholic families like the parents of Edmund Burke. The Burkes and Nagles were Old English families long established in North Cork: while the Burkes conformed, at least outwardly, the Nagles remained Catholic. A reminder of how brittle sectarian tensions could be was the execution of James Cotter, a prominent Catholic and Jacobite neighbour, on what were almost certainly trumped-up charges of rape, in 1720. As late as 1766, the celebrated execution of Fr Nicholas Sheehy in Co. Tipperary was a similar exercise in judicial murder. This was a nervous society.

It was also a traditional society where social relations relied on vertical ties of kinship and obligation, a kind of post-feudal world. In this respect, it was similar to most pre-industrial European societies. Like the Hiberno-Normans in earlier centuries, some post-Cromwellians went native, learned Gaelic and inter-married with older established families. This was the class that furnished the roaring, drunken, duelling squireens (memorably called the 'half-mounted gentlemen' by Jonah Barrington) who were very remote from anyone's idea of English gentility. But they helped to maintain social relations with their tenants, sponsoring hurling matches and race meetings, and their closeness to tenants and neighbours helped to dissolve some of the tensions mentioned above.

What no one in pre-industrial Europe could dissolve or avoid were subsistence crises: famines. They were a regular feature of Irish life throughout the century, although all of them seemed to pale into insignificance in the light of the last such crisis, the Great Famine of 1845–52. None the less, the most severe eighteenth-century famine, that of 1739–41, may have killed a greater proportion of the Irish population than its better remembered successor.

The winter of 1740 was the most severe of the century, so bitterly cold that Lough Neagh, the largest body of fresh water in the British Isles, froze solid so that men could walk safely across it from Co. Tyrone to Co. Antrim. Animals and birds died in great numbers; fish froze in rivers; and the potato crop, including the seed potatoes vital for the next year's planting, was ruined.

Which brings us back to Castletown and its folly. Old Speaker Conolly had died in 1729, but his widow Katherine remained the chatelaine of the great house until her death in 1752. When the famine struck in the winter of 1739 and then continued the following winter, she commissioned Richard Cassels (see chapter 18) to design the folly in order to provide famine relief work for the starving tenantry. Cassels was working on his designs for the neighbouring house at Carton, country seat of the earl of Leinster. What he designed is a remarkable structure: an obelisk standing on a triple-arched base with flanking mini-pavilions. It enclosed the long view from the rear of Castletown House.

Here we have the eighteenth century in symbolic miniature: the beautiful, symmetrical folly — useless but elegant, offering a distant perspective point for the delectation of the rich — put up as an act of kindly condescension by the architect *du jour* at the behest of the wealthiest woman in Ireland. And all to provide employment for starving tenants caught in nature's subsistence trap. Wealth and poverty, and too little between.

ENCLOSURE

This is a book about man-made constructions and artefacts and their effects upon Irish history. So why this photograph of the Irish countryside, so seemingly natural and timeless, without a building in sight? Because everything here is the work of man's hand: this landscape is as much a product of human intervention as any house or building or piece of engineering. The Irish countryside is beautiful because it is artificial.

Ancient Ireland was a vast forest. At the dawn of history, to quote one historian, 'a dense forest canopy covered the island so completely that a red squirrel could travel from ... Malin Head to Mizen Head ... without ever having to touch the ground'. In many respects, the story of Ireland's past has been the story of the clearing of the forests for agriculture. This has been a painstaking, piecemeal process from the earliest development of agriculture and has been carried on progressively in every age. It accelerated with the arrival of each wave of colonists and settlers. As we saw (chapter 14), the great earl of Cork stripped vast areas of forest to provide timber for his charcoal works: he was not the only seventeenth-century New English *arriviste* to do this.

By the early eighteenth century, the lowland forested areas had been substantially cleared and most available agricultural land was being farmed. For the greater part, it was subsistence agriculture: there was not yet a developed market in agricultural produce. Local markets did indeed exist, as is evidenced in place names such *Aonach Urmhumhan*, Nenagh, Co. Tipperary (the fair of Ormond). Even here, there is an ambiguity, because *aonach* meant both a fair and a place of assembly for recreation.

Local fairs and markets served local needs in the era before the development of fixed-shop retailing — itself greatly facilitated by the development of a national distribution system with the coming of the railways in the nineteenth century. They also were sufficient to the needs of subsistence, non-commercial agriculture. More developed markets, often focused on export, were confined to the larger urban centres, as butter in Cork and linen in Belfast.

The eighteenth century saw two major developments in the Irish countryside: the gradual move to commercial agriculture and a dramatic rise in the island's population, especially in the later decades. The commercialisation of agriculture was an improbable outworking of the Enlightenment. It meant bringing rational planning to the countryside, in an effort to increase efficiency and yields. It was one of the century's fads: an elite, top-down project encouraged by such worthy bodies as the Dublin Society (later the RDS, founded 1731). Its prescriptions were accurate: the effects of the commercialisation of agriculture achieved all that the improvers predicted. In the short run, however, it offended against the immemorial customs of the countryside and drew the wrath of a deeply conservative peasantry who — quite correctly — saw that an agricultural revolution was unlikely to benefit them.

Traditionally, most land had been held in common. Commonage was the norm in Ireland. Land was farmed by strip systems such as rundale, in which clusters of farming families had equal access to areas of open-field commonage, a system which was as fair as it was inefficient. In a part-subsistence economy like pre-modern Ireland — or many other pre-modern agricultural economies across Europe — fairness was more important than yields. But once agriculture is commercialised, yields become more important than fairness and the organisation of the land becomes a telling issue.

Enclosure meant the consolidation of strips of open-field farms into a single holding with a single owner, its boundaries marked by hedges, walls or fences. In England, the process had been proceeding erratically since the early sixteenth century. Its final surge came in the second half of the eighteenth and early nineteenth centuries, as the French and American wars — which effectively ran, with only limited respites, from 1756 to 1815 — hugely increased the demand for agricultural produce and put a premium on efficient production. Enclosed farms were more efficient, although perhaps not by as much as their promoters claimed — but their gains were bought at the price of social inequality. Where commonage had facilitated a rough equality of access to land, enclosure rewarded the larger tenants and the landlords and punished the poor.

In England, all enclosure had been a pretext for agrarian unrest. So it proved also in Ireland. The disadvantaged rural poor formed secret societies, of which the Whiteboys in Munster were the best-known and came to stand for similar groups elsewhere. In many respects, they were similar to the later Captain Swing revolt in England, where the rural poor rebelled against the development of a market-orientated rural economy, replacing the traditional 'moral economy' of mutual obligation and customary rights upheld by paternalistic landlords. In Ireland, however, all rural agitation was complicated by ethnic and confessional factors. There was still a strong sense of historical resentment against landlords whose titles were grounded in the Cromwellian confiscations and whose religion was not only alien but was a source of deep disaffection because of the legal obligation placed upon Catholic tenants to pay tithes for the upkeep of the Church of Ireland.

Most grievances were local and economic, so the agrarian secret societies never threatened to federate in a national movement — it was far too early for that, and the idea of a national political consciousness was yet to be born, although the elements for it lay scattered about. The societies were conspiracies of the powerless against the powerful and expressed themselves in gusts of anger: destruction of boundary markers, threats and intimidation, maiming of livestock. They succeeded in thoroughly frightening the landlords: the judicial murder of Fr Nicholas Sheehy in Clonmel in 1766 following a guilty verdict delivered by a local Protestant jury (after a Dublin jury had acquitted him) was one of the consequences of local establishment hysteria.

Enclosure has given us the typical field pattern of the modern Irish countryside, the domestic rural furniture that seems so familiar. It was not always so, and in historical time it is a relatively recent makeover. It also established the primacy of landlords and their bigger tenants in the rural pecking order, leaving the cottiers and landless labourers at maximum risk. The dramatic increase in population after 1780 was greatest among these latter groups but the instability of the situation was partly disguised by the ubiquity of the potato which provided a rich and easily cultivated source of protein. Until the catastrophic failure of the potato crop in the Great Famine of 1845–52, rural Ireland got away with it. But then came total catastrophe, as it was the poor who bore the brunt of starvation and emigration. Ironically, many landlords were ruined as well, leaving the stronger tenants in the best long-term position. It was their children and grandchildren who took possession of the land under the various land acts of the late nineteenth century that finally unpicked the Cromwellian settlement.

The controversies surrounding enclosure find a faint echo today in complaints about the EU's Common Agricultural Policy. It is designed to sustain small rural communities by central provision of subsidies to farmers who would otherwise be unable to compete in an open market. It draws the hostility of free traders — the modern equivalent of the rational, eighteenth-century enclosers and improvers — who deplore its support for agricultural inefficiency. The CAP stands for a version of moral economy, its opponents for cold science and rationality.

CATHOLIC CATHEDRAL, WATERFORD

The Cathedral of the Most Holy Trinity in Barrowstrand Street in Waterford was the first Catholic cathedral built in Ireland since the Reformation. Dating from 1793, its location is no accident. The south-east of Ireland, roughly everything east of a line drawn from Cork to Dublin, was the area where the Catholic interest survived best through the penal era that followed the Williamite victory of 1691.

Many Catholic families, dispossessed of their lands by Cromwell and his successors, went into trade and enriched themselves. This Catholic merchant class maintained its solidarity through inter-marriage and social reticence, not threatening the new established order. Sons were discreetly educated in Catholic schools abroad.

The Catholic church was strongest where the community was strongest. In the impoverished west of Ireland, it still remained a pre-modern peasant body. But in the south-east, in the rich river valleys and towns where the Old English Catholic middle class had survived the bad days in good order, church and community were strong. The simplest way to illustrate this is to look at the foundation dates of Catholic institutions. Apart from the cathedral in Waterford, to which we shall return, there was the opening of what is now Carlow College (also 1793), the first post-penal era institution of higher learning for Catholics in the country. The adjacent cathedral was begun in 1828, as was the parish church in Dungarvan, Co. Waterford. In nearby Youghal, Co. Cork, the parish church was built in 1798 in mock-Anglican style. In Cashel, Co. Tipperary, the church of St John the Baptist dates from 1790. Clongowes Wood College, the first Jesuit school in Ireland since the Reformation, opened in Co. Kildare in 1814. These are all very early foundation dates: most of the institutional revival of Catholicism in the rest of the island — especially in church-building — came in the second half of the nineteenth century.

The Catholic elite of the south-east were a generation or two ahead of the rest of their co-religionists in terms of their social cohesion, wealth and influence. It is no coincidence that so many leading figures in the nineteenth-century hierarchy came disproportionately from this region. Paul Cullen, the first ever Irish cardinal, who dominated the Irish church in the generation after the Famine, was from Ballitore, Co. Kildare. His nephew, Patrick Francis Moran, was cardinal archbishop of Sydney and a key figure in the Irish Catholic diaspora of the late nineteenth century. Cullen's predecessor as archbishop of Dublin, Daniel Murray, was born near Arklow, Co. Wicklow. John Warren Doyle, the formidable and influential bishop of Kildare & Leighlin in the 1820s, was from New Ross, Co. Wexford.

Similarly, it is remarkable how many of O'Connell's political lieutenants in the campaign for Catholic Emancipation came from the south-east. Thomas Wyse from Co. Waterford, who married a Bonaparte, was one such. Another was Richard Lalor Sheil from Co. Kilkenny. Denys Scully was from Kilfeakle, Co. Tipperary. All were hugely influential in their time; all came from wealthy backgrounds. Sheil and Scully were lawyers.

The wealth that sustained this community was nowhere better seen than in Waterford. The English agricultural improver and traveller Arthur Young noted in 1777 that the number of ships registered in Waterford had grown from fewer than thirty to more than eighty in the previous twenty years. Salt beef, butter and salt pork were the principal products traded from Waterford, with the port servicing almost 400 destinations from Britain to Scandinavia, the western Atlantic seaboard, the Caribbean and North America. In 1766, there were about 300 arrivals and departures from the port of Waterford; by 1771, a mere five years later, the equivalent number was 966.

John Roberts (1712–96) was the architect of Georgian Waterford. He was the son of one Thomas Roberts, also an architect whose background — unsurprisingly given the surname — was Welsh. After learning his trade in London, he came back to Waterford, where he lived for the rest of his life. He was engaged by the Anglican bishop of the city, Richard Chenevix, to complete the half-built Bishops' Palace, which he did. It made his reputation in the city.

He designed many splendid buildings in and around the city, including the City Hall. He was also responsible for the splendid church of St Iberius in Wexford and the Catholic church in Cashel mentioned above.

He designed both cathedrals in Waterford, Anglican and Roman Catholic, each a sensitive assertion in stone of the perceived virtues of the respective confessions. Christ Church, the Anglican cathedral, is all classical cool, chaste and restrained. The Catholic cathedral of the Most Holy Trinity is more exuberant, with hints of the Baroque. This perfectly captures the ascetic restraint of Protestantism and the theatricality of Catholicism: as exercises in architectural tact, in a country not always overflowing with it, these two beautiful churches take some beating.

What takes some believing is the capacity of the Catholic community of Waterford to fund their splendid new cathedral. But that is only so if you believe that the Catholic eighteenth century was a simply a time of unrelieved penal suppression and poverty. In fact, nearly all the penal laws were repealed in the last quarter of the century and in Waterford they hardly mattered anyway, since the Catholic community was in trade and not in land. This was a rich community. It could afford the splendours of Holy Trinity, just as — two generations later, in the adjacent county — the Catholics of Wexford could afford to engage Augustus Welby Pugin, no less, to design St Aidan's cathedral in Enniscorthy on the eve of the Famine.

All observers of late eighteenth-century Ireland agreed that its poorest parts were wretchedly poor. But that was not the whole story. Many Catholics of the south-east, in particular, were anything from comfortable, to well-to-do, to rich. This was a coherent, self-conscious community and it was from here that the leadership of Irish nationalism — an unblushingly confessional enterprise, despite the enlistment of the occasional virtuous Protestant to the cause — hailed. The Cathedral of the Holy Trinity in Waterford is evidence of a wealthy, cultivated, self-possessed community, fortunate in its generous architect, who has left this first major Catholic church of the post-penal era as a testament to his own talent and to the assurance of his patrons.

GREAT SOUTH WALL

The year 1707 is an important milestone in the story of Dublin. In that year, parliament passed 'An Act for Cleansing the Port, Harbour, and River of Dublin and for Erecting a Ballast Office in the said city'. The Ballast Office was the first municipal authority to take control of the port — it had been a prerogative of the crown until this moment — and it quickly made its presence felt.

The key functions of the Ballast Office were the imposition of port charges and the maintenance of the navigation channel, the latter a perennial problem. It also continued the progressive embanking of the river that had begun in earnest in the last quarter of the previous century. The construction of the quays on the north bank of the river, collectively to be known as the North Wall, was completed in less than twenty years. Charles Brooking's map of 1728 clearly shows a continuous embanking wall running from around the site of the modern Custom House to a point opposite Ringsend, roughly where the O_2 arena stands today. The East Wall was an extension of the North Wall following the line of the present East Wall Road around to Ballybough.

The North and East Walls required constant renewal and maintenance and were greatly improved in the nineteenth century when civil engineering skills were much advanced. But the construction of the originals in such an impressively short time was evidence of the energy which the early Ballast Office brought to the discharge of its duties. The leading traders and merchants of the city — they included such names as Humphrey Jervis, John Rogerson, William Fownes and John Eccles, all immortalised in street names — had an obvious material interest in improving the port.

They did not stop there. As early as 1715, they turned their attention to the south shore and began the construction of what was eventually to become the Great South Wall. Work started on this heroic project as early as 1716. The Ballast Office showed great consistency of purpose over a long period of time in the face of formidable practical difficulties. A wall of timbered piles was first laid down, pushing out towards what is now the Poolbeg lighthouse. By 1731, the basic structure was complete from the Pigeon House to the Poolbeg. A lightship marked the eastern end of the piles. It was a rickety and unsatisfactory structure in practice. The disturbance of wind and tides was often too much for the timber wall. Individual piles were displaced and the constant maintenance requirements were onerous. Moreover, the uncertain mooring of the lightship presented a near insoluble problem.

This in turn raised the question of a permanent lighthouse as the only effective substitute. The Ballast Office first proposed it in 1736. The idea got nowhere; it was raised again in 1744 with similar results. It was not until 1759 that the piles themselves were acknowledged to be an inadequate solution and the decision was taken to build a stone wall. The design incorporated a provision for a lighthouse foundation at the eastern end.

The abutment for the lighthouse foundation was built first and then construction of the wall proceeded from east to west, or back towards the city. It took over thirty years to carry the wall all the way up to the site of the present O'Connell Bridge but the lighthouse was finished and functioning as early as 1767.

The Great South Wall is not simply one of the finest engineering and construction achievements in the city's history. It is a testimony to the tenacity of purpose and consistency of vision of the city authorities through the entire length of the eighteenth century. A project that was a gleam in the eye in 1716 was not completed until the 1790s, by which time the Ballast Office, the original sponsoring body, had been replaced by a new Ballast Board (1786) and no one alive at the start had survived to see it finished.

The whole *raison d'être* of the Irish capital has always been seaborne trade. That was why the Vikings founded it in the ninth century. Yet the port had consistently presented problems: strongly tidal, leaving a shallow draught for shipping at low water; chronically prone to silting because of the effect of the tides on the two large sandbanks in the bay known as the North and South Bulls, thus churning the sands and dumping them in the shipping channel; and the consequent inability to establish secure landing places near to the city centre.

All these problems were eliminated or ameliorated by the building of the North, East and Great South Walls — and by the later addition of the North Bull Wall, jutting into the harbour from the Clontarf shore and creating a pinch point opposite the Poolbeg lighthouse at the end of the Great South Wall which produced a natural scouring and dredging effect on the ebb tide. In sum, these various walls and embankments made possible the modern development of the port of Dublin.

Of all these admirable engineering works, the Great South Wall was the finest, in that it faced the greatest and most formidable series of obstacles over a long period of time. It is in its way as fine a memorial to the city's golden age as any Georgian square or municipal building.

WHITE LINEN HALL, BELFAST

On 28 April 1783, the foundation stone was laid in central Belfast for the White Linen Hall. The building opened the following year. It was demolished in 1896 and on the site was built the present City Hall, the finest example of swaggering Victorian civic architecture in Ireland.

But we are concerned here not with what is but with what was. In the second half of the seventeenth century, the London parliament passed a number of Navigation Acts — usually in response to lobbies by influential English commercial interests — which placed certain restrictions on Irish trade. The export of live cattle from Ireland to England was banned in 1667 and the Irish woollen trade was disrupted by an act of 1699 which prohibited the export of wool to any country other than England. Although these and other measures were vexatious, and a rich source of grievance for the emerging 'patriot' interest in Ireland — that is, those Protestants who resented the inferior status of their kingdom implied by these acts — they were not as damaging to Irish trade as some contemporary writers asserted.

Indeed, the Irish wool trade prospered in the eighteenth century, even before the repeal of the 1699 act, helped by subterfuge and smuggling. The production of cloth and yarn was widespread in the country and the export trade — legal and illegal — continued. The manufacture of woollens was both a domestic and an industrial trade. Bigger volumes demanded the services of weavers in provincial towns. Once again, the rich south-east of the island was to the fore in this regard. But the real winners in all this were those products upon which no restrictions were placed by legislation. The rise of the provision trade in the south — butter, beef and bacon especially — and the linen trade in Ulster date from this period.

Linen had been cultivated in Ireland from ancient times. The growing and harvesting of flax was a backbreaking, labour-intensive business but it produced a linen cloth that could generate a variety of products from fine clothing to coarse sacking. The restrictions placed on the Irish woollen trade undoubtedly helped the development of linen from a purely domestic to a pre-industrial level. Irish linen represented no threat to any English interest, so no hostile legislation was applied to it. A Linen Board was established in Dublin in 1711; it encouraged innovation, gave grants to develop the industry and used its parliamentary influence to ensure favourable treatment for the product. The board aimed to spread the cultivation of flax right across the island — its members were drawn from all four provinces — but this ambition was never realised. The cultivation of flax and the manufacture of linen became focused on Ulster.

A key moment in this development was the arrival in Ireland in 1698 of Samuel-Louis Crommelin. Born in 1652, this French Huguenot had left his native land after the Revocation of the Edict of Nantes — which had offered toleration to French Protestants — in 1685. His arrival in Ireland was on the express invitation of King William III, who offered him the post of 'overseer of the royal linen manufacture of Ireland'. There was already a Huguenot community established at Lisburn, near Belfast, and Crommelin settled among them. The Huguenots brought the most advanced continental manufacturing techniques with them. Local landlords encouraged domestic production of flax as a cash crop that could supplement uncertain farm incomes.

When the Linen Board established a Linen Hall in Dublin in 1728, the overwhelming source of supply was Ulster. This is reflected in the naming of streets adjacent to the Linen Hall: Lisburn Street, Lurgan Street, Coleraine Street, Derry Street. The streets are still there but the building is long gone: it ceased to function in its original role in the 1820s and was taken over by the British army in the 1850s. In 1916, during the Easter Rising, it was occupied by forty unarmed members of the Army Pay Corps, who offered no resistance when it was invested by the rebels stationed in Reilly's pub (known thereafter as Reilly's Fort) on the far side of North King Street. Unable to hold it against counter-attack, they torched it. It burned for twenty-four hours.

As linen manufacture expanded in Ulster during the eighteenth century, technological advances developed to make the process more efficient. Not only was the work exhausting, it was frustratingly slow and time consuming. The development of water wheels on dammed rivers and streams mechanised the finishing process, thus saving human labour and speeding the time in which the linen drapers could deliver the finished product to market and turn it into cash.

The Ulster linen industry was most heavily focused in an area to the south of Lough Neagh known as the linen triangle. It ranged from Dungannon in the west to Lisburn in the east with the triangle forming its apex first at Armagh and later further south at Newry. The second half of the eighteenth century was a boom time for linen — despite a temporary slump in the 1770s — and local linen markets supplemented the Linen Hall in Dublin. In time, however, the greater distance involved in sending the product to be traded in Dublin prompted the building of the White Linen Hall in Belfast.

Ulster has always been different. For centuries, it was the least anglicised of the four provinces, in which the Gaelic lordships held unchallenged sway. Then, in the startling inversion of fortunes that followed the Flight of the Earls and the Plantation, it became the least Gaelic province: the large influx of Anglo-Scottish settlers gave it much of its modern character. From the nineteenth century on, the eastern half of the province, in particular, became the only part of Ireland touched by the industrial revolution. The expansion and local development of the domestic linen industry in the second half of the previous century had been a harbinger of this process. Ulster was growing less and less like the rest of Ireland. Visitors noticed the differences and remarked upon them. John Wesley, the founder of Methodism, who visited Ireland on twenty-one occasions from 1747, remarked as early as 1756, 'No sooner did we enter Ulster than we observed the difference. The ground was cultivated just as in England and the houses not only neat, but with doors, chimneys and windows.'

The White Linen Hall was a mark of that difference, of a localism that was bypassing

Dublin and finding its own mental and physical centre closer to home. The ancient Black Pig's Dyke — a series of prehistoric earthworks that girdled the southern reaches of the provinces and represented its line of defence — was being reconstituted in the minds of modern men.

Belfast City Hall.

MARKET HOUSE, GOREY

On the main street in Gorey, a market town in north Co. Wexford near the county border with Wicklow, stands the Market House. A simple five-bay classical structure, it was originally built in 1709. The current building is a modern replacement. This has been the civic centre of the town for almost 300 years. It has variously been a courthouse and a school and in modern times has accommodated the town council. It is a building of some charm and little real distinction, such as one might meet in any provincial town: discreet, tactful, unostentatious.

In the first half of 1798 it was a prison. This was where Anthony Perry was brought on 21 May on the orders of the local magistrates. Co. Wexford was in a state of suppressed hysteria, as much of Ireland had been since the abortive French landing in Bantry Bay in December 1796. Fifteen thousand crack revolutionary troops, units of the finest army in Europe, had almost effected a landing in a country ill-prepared to resist them. They had sailed on the orders of the French Directory — the revolutionary government — and thanks to the persuasive powers of Theobald Wolfe Tone.

Tone was a liberal Anglican lawyer, pamphleteer and political organiser. He was one of the founders of the Society of United Irishmen in 1791, a body reflecting the optimism of the early years of the French Revolution and dedicated to a republican, non-confessional secularism as a new basis for Irish identity and independence. This aspiration came up against older, entrenched confessional realities as the decade wore on. Sectarian tensions in southern Ulster between Catholics and Protestants — mainly Anglicans — led to the foundation of the Orange Order in 1795 and to the growth of the Defender movement among lower-class Catholics (see chapter 48). There followed a pitiless dragooning of Ulster by crown troops under General Gerard Lake in a search for arms; it bore far more heavily on Defenders than it did on Orangemen. Gradually, the anti-revolutionary hysteria spread south and the methods that had been deemed successful in Ulster were applied in Munster and Leinster.

The United Irishmen were well established in Co. Wexford but unlike Ulster, where the Orange–Defender division ran true along sectarian lines, there was a significant minority of liberal Protestants who supported the movement because of its French Revolutionary principles. Likewise, there was a significant minority of Catholics in the county, including all of the senior clergy, who were opposed to the United men and supported the crown.

Spies and raids by the military had all but disabled the United movement in Dublin, thus compromising the prospects for a planned national rising. This did nothing to restrain the zeal of crown forces at local level. In Co. Wexford, the North Cork Militia (most of them Catholics) was set to work. This zeal was not entirely misplaced. The United Irishmen had been plotting a rising with French support, but the latter did not materialise and the Dublin arrests threw all plans into confusion. In desperation, a pre-emptive attack was set for the night of 23 May 1798.

Martial law was declared in a number of counties and many atrocities were committed in the search for arms and for local leaders. On 27 April, Wexford was proclaimed and the Militia got to work. There followed the now familiar terror pattern: arbitrary arrests, house burnings and torture, including a new refinement known as pitch-capping, in which boiling pitch was applied to the victim's skull and set alight; by the time it set hard, it could only be detached by the unfortunate victim by pulling his hair and the skin of his scalp with it. The worst of this dragonnade focused on the north of the county, where the United movement was strongest and where sectarian tensions were more brittle than in the south.

Anthony Perry was a liberal Protestant landowner of some substance, farming near Inch, a village north of Gorey. He was also a leading member of the United Irishmen in the north Wexford/south Wicklow region. On the orders of the Wexford magistrates, he was arrested on 21 May and brought to the Market House in Gorey. It took the best part of five days to torture a confession out of Perry but the Militia men — prominent among them a particularly sadistic creature known as Tom the Devil — eventually succeeded. He did not reveal the names of all the United leaders in the county, but he revealed some of the most prominent.

He was released on 26 May, by which time the now enfeebled national rebellion had broken out and the United units in the county were mobilising. Despite his injuries, he joined the rebels and played an honourable part in the month-long struggle that ensued in Wexford. It ended on 21 June at Vinegar Hill, just above Enniscorthy in the centre of the county, with a crushing victory for Lake's crown troops over the United men. In that month — the bloodiest in modern Irish history — about 30,000 people died. Horrible atrocities were committed on both sides. While the crown troops made no pretence of having any ambitions other than repression and victory, the secular ideals of the United Irishmen did not always survive the fires of more traditional animosities: the rebels were guilty of a number of nakedly sectarian crimes against Protestant captives.

After Vinegar Hill, Perry and some others retreated north into the fastnesses of the Wicklow Mountains. He was eventually captured on 21 July at Edenderry, Co. Kildare, fleeing west towards Connacht with another leading Wexford rebel, the Catholic priest Mogue Kearns. They were hanged on the spot.

The Wexford rising of 1798 was a confused muddle of secular idealism, sectarian violence and pitiless government repression. Its effect on the minority of liberal Protestants in the county — and by extension, in the country — was chastening. Thereafter, the Protestant tradition in Ireland is overwhelmingly unionist and disinclined to flirt with secular republicanism. A similar effect was felt in Ulster, where a short-lived Presbyterian republican rebellion was crushed (given their democratic structures of church government, Presbyterians were drawn to republicanism more spontaneously than any other group in Ireland).

The year of liberty — 1798 — is often proposed as the fountainhead of a republican tradition that was secular, non-sectarian and central to all that followed. It was not. What emerged from the ashes was a theory not sustained in practice. Instead, the failure of secularism cast the nineteenth century in a confessional mould. The Orange Order proved to be the most enduring development of the 1790s. As for Irish nationalism, when it begins to mobilise in formidable numbers in the 1820s, it does so on a specifically confessional demand: Catholic Emancipation. Within a generation of 1798, Catholic unionists and Protestant nationalists were increasingly unrepresentative of their respective confessional communities. The immediate consequence of the rising was the passing of the Act of Union, the ending of the Irish parliament, and the creation of the United Kingdom of Great Britain and Ireland.

GLASNEVIN CEMETERY

John D'Arcy was killed by a fall from a horse in 1823. It was yet another unremarkable private tragedy, but its consequences were long felt and are with us to this day. D'Arcy was a Catholic and the owner of a substantial brewery in Dublin. His remains were brought to the cemetery of St Kevin for burial. St Kevin's was a Protestant cemetery in the western suburbs of the city, near Lower Kevin Street, itself named for the eponymous parish. There was no specifically Catholic cemetery in the city because of the penal laws but the practice was long established whereby Catholics and Dissenters could be buried in Anglican cemeteries. In the relatively relaxed atmosphere that obtained by the second half of the eighteenth century, confessional tensions were not intense as in earlier times or as they would become again following 1798.

When D'Arcy's remains were brought to St Kevin's for burial, the parish sexton, under orders from the archbishop of Dublin, Dr William Magee, refused permission to say Catholic prayers in the cemetery itself. The mourners were obliged to conduct the funerary rites outside the gates, in the street. This departure from customary practice was an interesting straw in the wind. Sectarian tensions were hardening. Accepted accommodations could no longer be taken for granted. The fact that a number of distinguished Catholics, including at least one Jesuit, had previously been buried in the cemetery with full Catholic graveside ritual was disregarded.

Magee was man of considerable reputation and ability. He grew up and was schooled in Co. Fermanagh. An intellectual of some contemporary reputation, he was successively professor of mathematics and Greek at Trinity and had held two previous sees prior to his appointment to Dublin in 1822. He was even seriously considered for an English bishopric, most unusually for an Irishman. However, like another formidable archbishop of Dublin from a south Ulster background — the Catholic John Charles McQuaid in the mid-twentieth century — he brought some of the sectarian animosities of his native province south. He was an obsessive anti-Catholic and he both engaged in and encouraged religious polemics. He was a strong supporter of the so-called 'Second Reformation', an attempt by Protestant evangelicals to effect a mass conversion of Irish Catholics in the 1820s.

In all this, a number of tributaries were flowing together. The heightened confessional tensions following 1798; the rise of evangelical Protestantism, with its missionary enthusiasms, in the early decades of the nineteenth century; and the contemporary development of Catholic nationalism under the leadership of Daniel O'Connell — all conspired to polarise Irish public life around confessional differences. Thus it was that when the remains of poor John D'Arcy were brought to the gates of St Kevin's cemetery in 1823, the stakes were raised in a manner that was deeply offensive to the mourners — and by extension, to the entire Catholic community.

This offence, gratuitously offered at the urging of Dr Magee, was the prompt for the establishment of a cemetery which was Catholic-owned and -controlled. As with any Catholic project in the 1820s, Daniel O'Connell was central to its purpose. During that decade, he agitated for and eventually secured the passage of Catholic Emancipation

(1829), which removed almost all the residual penal disabilities. In the course of this agitation, O'Connell developed the world's first organised mass mobilisation in a political cause and more or less invented modern Irish nationalism. The key moment was a by-election in Co. Clare in 1828 in which O'Connell himself stood and was elected, despite Catholics being then ineligible to sit in parliament. In effect, it was this victory that resulted in the change to the law.

The Clare by-election was drenched in the most uncompromising sectarian rhetoric: O'Connell knew his market. Although his rival, Vesey Fitzgerald, was a supporter of the Catholic cause and the son of a popular landlord who had himself been an opponent of the Act of Union, O'Connell played the two cards that were to sustain popular Irish nationalism for more than a century to come: faith and fatherland. He represented himself to the electors of Clare as one whose 'forefathers were for centuries the chieftains of the land and the friends of her people'. Describing Fitzgerald as 'the sworn libeller of the Catholic faith' — this because he had taken the oath of allegiance, anti-Catholic bits included, as all MPs were obliged to do — he drew the contrast with himself: 'one who has devoted his early life to your cause, who has consumed his manhood in a struggle for your liberties'. In effect, as one of O'Connell's biographers notes, his 'energies were directed to prising the peasant vote from the proprietors by the lever of religion'.

It was under O'Connell's leadership that a cemetery committee was established. It eventually purchased a 9-acre site in the townland of Prospect, to the north-west of the city close to the village of Glasnevin. This pleasant village, lying astride the River Tolka, had been a popular summer retreat for the well-to-do, of whom the most celebrated were Dr Patrick Delany and his wife Mary, whose house on the hill above the village, Delville, played host to Jonathan Swift on many occasions; the site is now occupied by the Bon Secours hospital. Glasnevin was and still is also the site of the National Botanic Gardens, then under the aegis of the Royal Dublin Society.

Prospect cemetery opened on 21 February 1832. The first burial was that of a four-year-old boy. The original name is still the official one but it is universally known as Glasnevin. Everyone in Dublin knows it by that name, whereas many would struggle to identify Prospect cemetery. It has grown to be the city's great necropolis, now expanded to cover more than 120 acres. O'Connell himself is buried there, in the most ostentatious vault in Ireland, over which stands a round tower memorial that is the visual focus of the cemetery and a vertical landmark visible from afar. Nearby is Parnell's grave, as chaste as O'Connell's is exuberant, topped by a boulder of Wicklow granite. Although formally non-sectarian, Glasnevin became de facto the Catholic burial ground and grew to be one of the city's greatest Victorian legacies. Most Catholic archbishops of Dublin are buried here, some in dramatic monuments just inside the main gates, of which G.C. Ashlin's memorial for Cardinal McCabe (1885) is the most elaborate. The Hades episode in Joyce's *Ulysses* concludes here, as Paddy Dignam is laid to rest. The republican plot holds the graves of many leaders and victims of the independence struggle. The cemetery contains the remains of the great and the ordinary, as well as of the indigent poor: in addition to Famine victims from the 1840s, there were over 11,000 victims of the 1849 cholera epidemic buried here in that year alone. In all, more than 1.5 million dead lie here.

Glasnevin cemetery marks the rise of Catholic power. If, in the eighteenth century, one spoke of the Irish Nation, one meant and was understood to mean the nation of the Protestant ascendancy with its parliament in College Green and its control of all the country's levers of power. By the 1830s, when Glasnevin opened its gates, the Irish Nation meant the organised movement of Catholics to loosen or break the connection to Great Britain, a project that waxed and waned through the century before achieving most of its aims in 1922. Lord John George de la Poer Beresford (1773–1862), Church of Ireland archbishop of Armagh, summed it up in simple language: 'When I was a boy "the Irish people" meant the Protestants; now it means the Roman Catholics.'

NEWTOWNBARRY

The Cloideach, anglicised as Clody, is a stream that flows from Mount Leinster in Co. Carlow and joins the Slaney just inside the county border with Wexford. This part of Ireland had been in the possession of the Kavanagh family for centuries, but they were dispossessed after the Williamite wars and joined the exodus of the Wild Geese to France. The land passed into the ownership of New English families and in 1719 came into the possession of James Barry, the sheriff of the city of Dublin, who developed a town here. The site had previously been called Bun Cloideach, the mouth of the Cloideach, or in anglicised form Bunclody. Here James Barry developed an estate town which he named for himself: Newtownbarry.

Estate towns are dotted all over Ireland. They are the product of paternalistic planning of a kind often absent in Irish towns, most of which developed randomly and in immediate response to circumstance, without any obvious coherence or architectural unity. Estate towns, with their rational self-assurance, are one of the benign legacies of the eighteenth century. They represent urban order, if only in micro.

Yet urban order or no, Newtownbarry was the scene of a deadly affray on 18 June 1832. Here, on the seventeenth anniversary of the battle of Waterloo, a company of yeomanry fired into a crowd at a part of the town called the Pound. Seventeen people died and twenty were injured. The cause of this incident was the so-called Tithe War.

Tithes were a tax — notionally one-tenth of earnings — levied either in cash or kind for the upkeep of the clergy of the established Church of Ireland, whose congregations constituted barely 10 per cent of the entire Irish population. Tithes had always been resented and had been the proximate cause of sporadic campaigns of agrarian violence ever since the 1760s. These campaigns had escalated in the early 1830s, resulting in serious violence in the countryside. In general, attempts to enforce payment — or worse, to distrain goods for non-payment — met with fierce resistance.

Resistance to payment had been sporadic among Catholics since the 1760s. But in the period of heightened expectation following Catholic Emancipation, the sense of grievance turned to outright resistance. By the 1830s, almost two-thirds of the total income of the Church of Ireland came from tithes. Given this level of dependence, it was not an issue easily resolved. At the same time, it was a chronic source of grievance among people not in communion with the Church of Ireland, upon whom fell the main burden of payment. Moreover, from 1735 until 1823 pasturage was excluded from the scheme, which meant that the best land was exempt. Given the reality of land-holding patterns, this meant that wealthy members of the Church of Ireland paid less than their due proportion for the upkeep of their own church, while the principal burden fell on poorer Catholics and — in Ulster — Presbyterians.

The 'Tithe War' started in Graiguenamanagh, Co. Kilkenny in October 1830 when the cattle of the parish priest, Fr Martin Doyle — a relation of the formidable Bishop James Warren Doyle of Kildare & Leighlin — were distrained for non-payment. A campaign of non-payment first spread throughout South Leinster and Munster: once again, this critical region was in the van of modernisation. Eventually 22 of the 32 counties in Ireland were involved. Although formally a campaign of passive resistance, it inevitably turned violent.

The use of police and troops to distrain goods and livestock resulted in serious clashes. The deaths at Newtownbarry resulted from a riot when distrained cattle were sold off to settle unpaid tithes. Nor was this an isolated, or even an exceptional, incident: less than three weeks earlier, on 31 May, another seventeen people were killed by troops in Castlepollard, Co. Westmeath, in similar circumstances. In October, the government was sufficiently alarmed to pass the Tumultuous Risings Act, which substituted transportation for execution for certain capital crimes: it was thought — perhaps correctly — to be a greater deterrent. None the less, on 14 December, a mob of 2,000 people attacked troops at Carrickshock, Co. Kilkenny, about 40km south-west of Newtownbarry, during a tithe riot: 16 died.

In all, over 43,000 decrees were issued against defaulters, while Lord Gort claimed in 1832 that the anti-tithe campaign had resulted to date in 242 homicides; 1,179 robberies; 401 burglaries; 568 burnings; 280 cattle maimings; 161 assaults; 203 riots and 723 attacks on houses. The withdrawal of police and the yeomanry from tithe enforcement duties in 1833 took much of the heat out of the situation, but by now the total arrears were more than £1 million. In effect, London gifted this sum to the Church of Ireland — an open acknowledgment that the traditional tithe system was no longer viable.

The tithe question was not settled by legislation until 1838, when O'Connell — who had kept his distance from the agitation while benefiting politically from it (he was not the last Irish nationalist to master this trick) — formed a proposal which would mean the state taking over responsibility for clerical payments, while a local tax would be levied in support of the newly formed Irish Constabulary. The proposal was broadly adopted by the government and, although much watered down in the House of Lords, was carried. The net effect was to convert the tithes into a rent charge, making them invisible. The hated tithe proctors, who had conducted the assessments and collected the tithes, disappeared from the land. With them went the visible reality of the problem itself.

Newtownbarry in the 1830s represented the twin faces of post-Williamite Ireland. The planned estate village, an image of Enlightenment order, but underneath the surface a seething sense of dispossession and resentment. For most of the eighteenth century, the resentment of the Catholic majority was of no political or social account. It was a world of sullen impotence. But in the early decades of the nineteenth century, a specifically Catholic community consciousness formed. While it absorbed the idea of popular sovereignty from the French Revolution, it located it in an older Irish sense of confessional solidarity — one that went back at least to the 1640s, if not to the Reformation itself — so that the project that we know as Irish nationalism became an overwhelmingly Catholic one.

MOIRA RAILWAY STATION

ost of the passengers on the frequent Enterprise services which link
Dublin and Belfast will scarcely notice Moira station as their express
train hurtles through at high speed. However, the main station building
at Moira is a remarkable relic, largely unaltered since the 1840s, a link
to the earliest days of the railway age in Ireland.

From our perspective in the second decade of the new millennium, it is hard to
appreciate just what a revolution the coming of the railways brought in its wake in the

middle of the nineteenth century. Mankind could travel at speeds hitherto undreamed of and goods could be transported relatively cheaply and quickly over distances which would have been economically unthinkable only a few years before. But more than that, for many Victorians of varying degrees of eminence, the railway seemed to express the very spirit of the age, the embodiment of that great watchword of the era: progress. Ally that with the potential for great profits and it is easy to understand the enthusiasm with which this new means of transport was embraced on both sides of the Irish Sea.

This led to a flurry of railway promotions in the 1830s, a decade which saw the opening of Ireland's first railway, that from Dublin to Kingstown in 1834. This first Railway Mania, as it was called, predictably ended in tears when an economic slump brought the collapse of many highly speculative schemes. The result was the ruination of the investors in these schemes. In Ireland, just one of the many railway companies launched in the 1830s had managed to start running a train service by the end of the decade. That was the Ulster Railway Company, which opened the first part of its projected line from Belfast to Armagh down the Lagan Valley to connect the city to Lisburn on 12 August 1839.

With the railway to Lisburn open, in the spring of 1840, the UR awarded a contract worth £90,000 for the next part of their line, from Lisburn to Portadown, to a man whose name would be synonymous with the construction of the Irish railway network, William Dargan. He was already well known in Belfast, where in 1839 he started work on dredging a new deep water channel to allow larger vessels to access the port. The mud and soil excavated was used to create what was at first known as Dargan's Island but later, after a royal visit, was renamed the Queen's Island, the future home of the shipbuilders Harland & Wolff and now chiefly remembered as the birthplace of the ill-fated *Titanic*.

Work on the extension of the railway proceeded apace. Part of the new line was temporarily opened in July 1841 as far as the Maze to bring passengers to the race meetings held there. Over 18,000 racegoers used the trains during the week of the races. Services from Belfast were extended to run to Lurgan from 18 November 1841 and to a temporary terminus at Seagoe on the outskirts of Portadown on 31 January 1842. To coincide with the extension of train services to Lurgan, a station was opened at Moira between Lisburn and Lurgan to serve the nearby village. At first only a single track was laid, so to enable trains in either direction to cross each other a passing loop was provided at Moira. When the line was being built, many thousands of skeletons of both men and horses were unearthed. These were linked to a battle which took place in 637 AD. Some historians of this remote and poorly documented era claim that the battle of Mag

Roth/Moira was the biggest ever fought on Irish soil. The evidence unearthed by William Dargan's navvies would give some credence to this assertion.

Like many Irish stations, Moira's was some distance from the place it purported to serve, the village being about a mile away. One geographical quirk about the station is that it is actually located in Co. Antrim though the village it serves is in Co. Down. However, when you had a virtual monopoly of traffic, as the railways did until the rise of the internal combustion engine in the post-World War I era, this was not a concern for the railway companies. Passengers and goods had to come to you; there was no realistic alternative. The building of the M1 motorway, which runs parallel to the railway here, in the 1960s served to distance the line from the village even more. The motorway also consigned to history another transport artery which had served Moira before the coming of the Ulster Railway, the Lagan Navigation. Construction of this waterway to link Belfast to Lough Neagh began in 1756 but was not completed until 1794. The canal finally closed in the 1950s and the central section, between Sprucefield and Moira, was largely obliterated by the construction of the motorway. Just beyond Moira station a bridge carries the railway over the remains of the canal.

The main station building at Moira was constructed to an Italianate design of the UR's engineer, John Godwin. It is the last original UR station in existence and one of the oldest in Ireland. It has been little altered since the 1840s. The station lost its staff and became a request stop in the 1960s. The level crossing at the Belfast end was automated in the 1980s, allowing the signal box to be closed, though it has been preserved by the station's current owners, Northern Ireland's Department of the Environment, who are also to be praised for the excellent condition of the historic and unique station building.

When the line first opened, Moira was served by six trains in each direction on weekdays and three on Sundays. In 1922 there were nine services to and from Belfast on weekdays but only one on Sundays. By 1950 the number of trains had increased to sixteen from Belfast on weekdays and six on Sundays, with thirteen and five respectively in the other direction. Today, the service provided by Northern Ireland Railways is better than it has ever been with over thirty trains a day, in each direction, calling there on weekdays. Though the facilities for passengers at Moira today are much more utilitarian than those provided by the UR and the original station is no longer used by travellers, the frequency and speed of the train service is something which those Victorian railway promoters could never have envisaged when they built the line and the station in the 1840s.

ENGLISH MARKET, CORK

The English Market in Cork is one of the sights of the city and is beyond any question the finest food market in Ireland. Nothing else comes close. The present splendid enclosure dates from 1862, although it required significant restoration and re-development following serious fires in 1980 and 1986. None the less, the basic integrity of Sir John Benson's original design has been triumphantly retained and the market has won a Europa Nostra award for architectural preservation.

All this is to the great credit of the Cork city authorities and is as it should be. For Cork has a long and distinguished reputation as a centre of the provision trade. The English Market did not just happen. As with everything, there is a context and a backstory.

The market was established in 1788. At first, it catered to the more prosperous elements in the city. This distinguished it from the Irish Market, on the far side of Patrick Street off North Main Street, where prices were generally lower. This English/Irish distinction echoed similar contrasts in the names of districts, as in Limerick (see chapter 19), where English Town meant the older, more central and more 'civic' area while Irish Town was a rougher suburb, usually outside the city walls. Any Irishtown in any Irish town generally runs true to this sharp difference.

Following the devastating Desmond wars and the settlement of New English landowners in Munster in the late sixteenth and early seventeenth centuries, the province recovered and prospered with impressive speed. The port of Youghal controlled most of the trade to the west of England, Kinsale was a major importer of tobacco — for which the Irish market seemed insatiable — and Cork itself had a vigorous trade with the continent. Over time, Cork eclipsed the smaller ports and became the dominant regional entrepôt. The greater geographical range of Cork's maritime trade was very marked: in the 1680s, only a quarter of its trade was with England, almost as much as it was doing with the Caribbean islands, whereas the greatest proportion was with France, the Low Countries and the Iberian peninsula.

By 1700, Cork had taken advantage of its central location in south Munster and the size of its natural outer harbour to overwhelm smaller ports from Dungarvan to Dingle. It was a major export point for wool, still a significant element of Irish trade. But as the eighteenth century wore on, it was the provision trade that came more and more to dominate the commerce of the southern capital. Until about 1750, the principal commodities in the city's trade were beef, butter and woollens in that order. The second half of the century — the period in which the English Market was first established — saw a dramatic expansion. The beef trade, in particular, flourished. Even in the early part of the century, Cork controlled more than 40 per cent of the Irish export market; by the second half, its regional dominance had grown so overwhelming as to be nearly total. The concentration of slaughterhouses and abattoirs in the city was also a factor in this dominance.

As with beef, so went the butter trade, although not to the same volume or degree. Youghal had been a major port of departure for salted butter but had lost this advantage to Cork by 1700. Once again, export markets were diverse and in some instances far-flung, so that the city's commercial bets were spread over the widest possible number of customers: if one market failed for any reason — war was a frequent cause of problems — another could be exploited in its stead.

The commercial trade in salted beef and butter reached its apogee in the 1760s. Thereafter the nature of the trade changed, and much of this change was driven by war. War is famously bad for commerce and Britain was at war with France (and for a time, with its American colonies, who had French assistance) more or less continuously from the start of the Seven Years' War in 1756 until the battle of Waterloo in 1815. Intervals of peace were blessed remissions, but the whole period — the span of two adult lifetimes — was a time of international conflict.

For one of the biggest centres of the provision trade in Europe, located on the western margins of one of the principal combatants, the wars brought unprecedented prosperity. Ireland became the bread basket of the British forces and Cork was the port with the most developed supply infrastructure. (This was a theme that repeated itself in World War I, when the most cogent British argument *against* imposing conscription in Ireland was not political, but practical: young men employed in agriculture were of more benefit on the farm than at the front.)

The long series of wars from 1756 to 1815 brought high prices for the staples that sustained Cork's prosperity: beef and butter, as we have seen, and now increasingly pork and bacon. In relative terms, beef lost its pre-eminence from its high point in the 1760s; by the 1790s, it had fallen to a level equal to pigmeat in terms of the quantities exported through Cork. Pork and bacon, in turn, had risen from a low base and while never approaching the quantities achieved by beef exports in earlier decades became the leading export meat commodity early in the nineteenth century. The rise of pork was a direct consequence of the war. The demand for pork from the military increased spectacularly. The relative ease with which pork can be salted and preserved is a consideration here but so is price, although the gap in cost between pork and beef narrowed over time.

The restored Victorian splendour of the English Market might lead one to suppose that here is a monument to nineteenth-century retail developments. It is all that, but more besides. It renews a tradition that is older than the market itself; that marked Munster and Cork as the centre of the Irish provision trade, which in turn was a key factor in Britain's rise to empire. It is little surprise that the English Market is here and not somewhere else, or that the capital of Irish gastronomy is just down the road in Kinsale, or that Ballymaloe House a few kilometres to the east has been the greatest single influence in transforming modern Irish attitudes to food, or that so many world-class cheeses are being developed in the region. Traditions die hard.

WORKHOUSE

I n medieval times, poor relief was a matter for the church. But in Tudor England the expansion of the secular state — which entailed the subordination of the state church and the dissolution of the monasteries — meant that it assumed direct responsibility in this area for the first time. The first English Poor Law was enacted in 1536. Subsequent reforms and additions followed over the centuries, with the workhouse system introduced in 1723. Eventually a New Poor Law Act of 1834 created 600 unions of parishes in which poor relief was only available to those prepared to enter a workhouse. Conditions in the workhouses were kept deliberately harsh to deter all but the destitute poor from applying.

In Ireland, a Commission of Enquiry into the Poor Law was established in 1833, its members being well acquainted with Irish conditions and including both the Church of Ireland and the Roman Catholic archbishops of Dublin. It recommended a series of reforms and counselled against a simple extension of the English law to Ireland. Their report was ignored by the government, which instead despatched George Nicholls, an English Poor Law commissioner who had no intimate knowledge of Irish conditions, to review the situation. Nicholls — yet another Englishman who knew what was best for the creoles — did as he was implicitly bid, and the English act was extended to Ireland by statute in 1838.

It established a network of 130 Poor Law unions, each centred on a market town in which a workhouse was to be built. As in England, no relief for poverty or distress was available outside the dreaded workhouses: you had to enter in order to benefit. The scheme was financed by a local rate paid jointly by landlords and the more substantial tenants.

Then came the catastrophe that overwhelmed the system and that overwhelmed Ireland itself.

In June 1845, a new and mysterious potato blight appeared for the first time. It resulted in the loss of about one-third of the potato harvest that year. It was a crisis but not a disaster. The blight had appeared late in the year and much of the crop was already harvested when it struck. But then there was a wholesale failure of the potato crop in the summer of 1846. The blight re-appeared earlier that year, before any harvesting could begin. This was the real beginning of the Great Famine.

The Whig government led by Lord John Russell was doctrinaire in its espousal of free trade principles and was disinclined to sanction direct state relief. The distress of the previous year had clearly left parts of the Irish population in a poor position to cope with the shattering effects of total potato failure. The government reduced grain importation into Ireland and attempted to run down public works schemes. These schemes had been introduced without fuss, because by offering outdoor relief they breached a key provision of the Poor Law, upon which the government wished to throw the whole burden of famine relief. These efforts were augmented by private schemes such as the soup kitchens provided by the Quakers, a community that performed heroically during the Famine.

Almost 500,000 desperate people were employed in public works by the end of 1846 and nearly half as many again three months later. But London's heart was not in it. The government's strategic aim was to minimise its own direct involvement in famine relief and make Ireland responsible for the cost, which was to be borne by Irish landlords and the Poor Law system. This strategy was grounded in an assertion that a local crisis should be treated locally and should not become a burden on national finances.

It was an article of faith in Westminster that Ireland was a social and economic mess. Its landlords were feckless and reactionary, ignoring the modernising improvements that had transformed English agriculture. The tenants were regarded as a slothful human mass kept in a permanent state of backward subsistence by their reliance on the potato. The doctrinaire free traders wanted a wholesale shakeout of Irish agriculture: enclosure, modernisation, assisted passage schemes for tenants who were surplus to requirements, and so on. In their eyes, the Famine was the inevitable consequence of this situation and a providential opportunity to remedy it.

After the failure of 1846, people were reduced to eating seed potatoes. Ironically, the crop did not fail in 1847 but yields were low because so little had been sown. Black '47 entered the folk memory. People were not simply dying of starvation but also of the illnesses induced by starvation, especially typhus and relapsing fever. Vast hordes of sick and dying wandered the countryside, throwing themselves onto the workhouses, which proved utterly inadequate to the task. The Poor Law was shouldering a burden it had never been intended to bear.

The rise in mortality and distress in 1847 was overwhelming. The scaling down of public works left the poorest people destitute, so that many had no money to buy such grain as was available for purchase. The worse things got, the less local agencies could cope. The more landlords were stretched, the tougher the line they took with tenants unable to keep up their rental payments. Evictions increased, throwing ever more wretched, destitute and starving families on to the roads.

This process was accelerated in turn by a piece of legislation known as the Quarter-Acre Clause. The Poor Law Extension Act 1847 stated that 'occupiers of more than a quarter-acre of land are not to be deemed destitute, nor to be relieved out of the poor rates'. Thus starving peasants were faced with the need to surrender their tiny holdings in order to qualify for poor relief. Naturally, those who did so never recovered them. Then the potato crop failed again in 1848. It was another catastrophic failure, as in 1846. The government made further poor relief dependent on the collection of arrears in the Poor Law rates. Nearly £1m was duly collected but at the cost of growing agrarian unrest. The workhouses were full to overflowing; the Poor Law system effectively collapsed. Emigration beckoned for many. Landlords faced ruin. There were further minor failures of the potato crop up until 1852, although the worst of the devastation was over by 1849.

The 1851 census told the story simply. The population of Ireland had been reduced by 20 per cent in a decade, a loss of over 1.5 million people. Of these, at least half died; the rest emigrated. Emigration became a way of life from then on, causing the population to decline to less than 4.4 million in 1911. In seventy years, the span of a single life, the population of Ireland was almost cut in half.

The Famine was a natural ecological disaster. The government's response turned the disaster into a catastrophe. Almost a million people died. Millions more emigrated, many taking with them a hatred of Britain for letting Ireland starve. The last great subsistence crisis in Europe occurred in a part of the richest country in the world and its effects were made more severe than they otherwise might have been by the choices of that country's government.

ST ENOCH'S, BELFAST

D aniel O'Connell mobilised the Catholics of the three southern provinces in support of his campaigns for Catholic Emancipation and Repeal of the Union. The first succeeded; the second failed. In the process, he created Irish democracy. But O'Connell had a blind spot about the northern province — not that he was the last Irish nationalist of whom that could be said — and he only ever made one visit there, in 1841.

Ulster had a Protestant majority. It was not a united community. Tensions between members of the established Church of Ireland (Anglican), mainly of English descent, and the Presbyterians of Scots descent were very marked. The liberal impulse in Presbyterianism, with its instinct for democracy, had found expression in 1798. Although much chastened thereafter, it took time for this liberal Presbyterian tradition to die. But by the 1840s, it was increasingly under challenge.

Presbyterianism, with its highly literate congregations, was a fertile ground for theological disputation. In the first half of the nineteenth century, conservative and orthodox subscribers to the Westminster Confession of Faith — the foundation document of the Church of Scotland — gradually marginalised the so-called non-subscribers within Ulster. In broad political terms, it was a victory for conservatives and evangelicals over those of a more liberal, accommodating temper.

The one thing that united all Ulster Protestants, whether Church of Ireland or any shade of Presbyterian, was suspicion and dislike of Catholics. The antagonism ran long and deep, right back to original Plantation days, and it had never abated. It was no coincidence that the swing to conservatism in Presbyterianism coincided with the growing advance of Catholic interests under O'Connell.

In 1828, during the Catholic Emancipation campaign and thirteen years before his own visit, O'Connell had approved an initiative by one of his more maverick allies, Honest Jack Lawless, to try to extend the reach of the Catholic Association to Ulster. This initiative was known by the revealing title of 'the invasion of Ulster', Honest Jack's own formulation. He led a large crowd north but was repulsed by a formidable gathering of Orangemen in Ballybay, Co. Monaghan. It was the first town on the southern reaches of Ulster where Protestants felt confident enough to muster in serious numbers. Lawless wisely backed off. Humiliatingly, that was as far as things went for the 'invasion' force: in the face of the first concentrated Ulster Protestant resistance to a nationalist initiative, all they could do was to retreat.

When, therefore, O'Connell arrived in Belfast in January 1841 to address a Repeal meeting, he knew he was entering hostile territory. Indeed, he had to travel incognito to avoid Orange mobs. He required police protection and the windows of his hotel were stoned. He was challenged to a public debate by Rev. Henry Cooke, the leading conservative Presbyterian clergyman, but he uncharacteristically declined. Cooke had established himself as the most formidable champion of traditional Presbyterianism. He stands at the head of the Ulster Presbyterian tradition in its modern form.

Cooke had a formidable intellect and was staunchly conservative, but he was no demagogue. The same could hardly be said for the two other best remembered Protestant controversialists of the nineteenth century, Thomas Drew and Hugh Hanna. Drew was the low-church Anglican incumbent of Christ Church, College Square, Belfast. Hanna, an evangelical Presbyterian, acquired such a reputation as an incendiary sectarian preacher that eventually, in 1870, he had St Enoch's built for his congregation at Carlisle Circus, at the southern end of the Antrim Road. It was the largest Presbyterian church in a largely Presbyterian city.

By then, Drew and Hanna had made their mark on the city's life. In 1857, Drew's sermon at a 12 July Orange commemoration tripped off a sectarian riot that lasted ten days and inaugurated one of Belfast's uglier recurring traditions: major riots followed regularly, the worst of them in 1864, 1872 and 1886, not to mention what was to come in the twentieth century. Hugh Hanna had also made his mark as a firebrand asserting the most uncompromising Protestant values and railing against Catholicism, this in a city in which the Catholic population — many of them Famine and post-Famine migrants from the countryside come to the city for work — was growing apace. When he appeared before a commission investigating the 1857 riots, Hanna was asked if he would preach knowing that his words would foment a riot. He replied, 'I would, sir. Our most valuable rights have been obtained by conflict.'

Both Drew and Hanna were enthusiastic supporters of the Ulster Revival of 1859. This was an outbreak of populist piety or religious hysteria — take your pick according to preference — in eastern Ulster. It affected all Protestant denominations. As with all such manifestations, it emphasised conversion, personal re-birth and salvation, visions and forms of irrational excess. It re-asserted fundamental Calvinist values, appealing to the most demotic and bigoted kind of anti-Popery, with which the city was already well supplied. Its emotional excesses drove it ever farther from the tradition of intellectual Presbyterianism, which was the principal victim first of Cooke's conservatism and now of this evangelical fervour.

St Enoch's was designed in a Victorian mock-Gothic style, not unlike many of the Catholic churches being built around Ireland at the time. It originally had a fleche spire, which was later removed. The interior was designed to Hanna's specifications and could accommodate up to 2,000 congregants. It was no accident that the biggest congregation in Belfast gravitated to the church of a sectarian firebrand preacher in an age when political and religious differences were so intense.

During the home rule crisis of 1886, the rioting in Belfast became so bad that extra RIC recruits were drafted in from around the country. The fact that many of these were southern Catholics, and that one company which was trapped by an enflamed mob on the Shankill Road fired into the crowd and killed seven people, gave Hanna ample cause for conspiracy theories when he addressed his congregation from the pulpit of St Enoch's the following Sunday. In his interpretation of events, what had happened was simple: the home rule bill had just been defeated; a loyal crowd was celebrating victory (and looting the contents of a wrecked liquor store, something that Rev. Hanna unaccountably neglected to mention) yet the forces of the government that had tried to betray the people's trust were now killing them in the street. Hanna did not invent Protestant sectarian paranoia but he did nothing to retard its progress.

Roaring Hugh Hanna, as he was known, died in 1892. Two years later, a statue of him in his preaching robes was erected outside St Enoch's. It became an early victim of the post-1968 Troubles when it was blown up in 1970. St Enoch's itself, by then much reduced from the days of its pomp, was destroyed in an arson attack in 1985 and not re-built. A proposal to re-erect Hanna's statue in the 1990s was deemed too provocative.

AVONDALE

The Parnell family originated in Cheshire. Thomas Parnell, whose uncle and grandfather had each been mayor of Congleton, was a beneficiary of the Cromwellian plantation. Whether he had supported the parliamentary cause in the civil war with money or in arms is unclear, but he secured an estate in Queen's County (Laois) and settled to life as a country gentleman. That was in the 1660s.

A number of descendants distinguished themselves, but the first to make an impact on Irish public life was Sir John Parnell, who rose to be Chancellor of the Irish Exchequer. He was a principled opponent of the Act of Union, a fact that did no harm to his great-grandson's political prospects, but like many opponents of the Union he was no friend to Catholic ambitions. One of his sons, William Parnell, inherited the house and estate at Avondale, Co. Wicklow, in 1795, from a cousin, Samuel Hayes, whose family was inter-married with the Parnells. The house dated from 1777. In turn, his son John Henry Parnell inherited it and lived there with his American wife, Delia Stewart. She was the daughter of Admiral Stewart — Old Ironsides — who had distinguished himself during the war with the British in 1812.

Charles Stewart Parnell was born here in 1846. He was reared in the manner of an Irish country gentleman, sent first to a girls' school in Somerset and later to a private academy in Oxfordshire, both of which he hated. In 1865, he went to Cambridge but was expelled before taking his degree. Back in Wicklow his chief preoccupation was cricket, at which he cheated. All in all, it was an unlikely background for a leader of Irish nationalism.

On 1 September 1870 the Home Government Association was launched in Dublin by Isaac Butt, a barrister and former MP. Its basic demand was for some form of devolved autonomy for Ireland or, in the brilliantly vague term in which it couched the demand, home rule.

The term was deliberately elastic. In the early days, in Butt's formulation, it amounted to a call for devolved domestic parliaments for Ireland, Scotland and England (but not for Wales). Westminster would remain sovereign and would deal with foreign and imperial matters. Part of home rule's early appeal lay with some members of the Church of Ireland who felt betrayed by the disestablishment of their church in 1869 and who thought that a Dublin parliament could be a better safeguard for Protestant interests. Butt himself was a conservative Protestant.

As the 1870s wore on, the home rule movement took on a more overtly nationalist hue. Constitutional nationalists and ex-Fenians were drawn to it; it also attracted the support of parish clergy, although not yet of the hierarchy. In the 1874 general election that ousted Gladstone and installed Disraeli, candidates pledged to home rule won 59 seats. But they did not constitute a party in any modern sense. Butt was a gentlemanly but ineffective leader; he lost the support of many of his original Protestant adherents without gaining the confidence of the Catholic hierarchy; and the Fenian and neo-Fenian element among his MPs were effectively out of his control. From 1876 on, they began disruptive filibustering tactics in Westminster.

The Fenians, otherwise the Irish Republican Brotherhood (IRB), had been founded in 1858 as a secret, revolutionary, republican separatist group. They represented the radical strand in Irish nationalism, committed to armed revolution and uninterested in the inevitable compromises of parliamentary politics. They tended to attract the support in disproportionate numbers of ambitious urban lower-middle-class men, people bent on change and self-improvement. They attempted a rising in 1867 that was more farce than tragedy. This caused some Fenians to revise their previous hostility to parliamentary politics, which explained the presence of some of their number among Butt's party at Westminster.

Parnell was elected MP for Co. Meath in 1875 and within a few years had displaced Butt as leader of the Irish party. Moreover, he had made influential Fenian friends. In 1877, Michael Davitt from Co. Mayo was released from prison after serving a seven-year sentence for Fenian activities. The next year, in New York, he agreed a programme with John Devoy, the leading Irish-American nationalist, called the New Departure. It meant that republicans, parliamentarians and agrarian radicals would co-operate. This led to the foundation of the Land League in 1879. Parnell as leader in parliament and Davitt as head of the Land League made a formidable coalition. The campaign for land reform — first for tenant rights, later for outright tenant ownership — convulsed the country in the early 1880s and set in train a process that eventually destroyed the Cromwellian land settlement.

The Liberals under Gladstone returned to power at Westminster in 1880 and passed a major Land Act the following year which conceded some of the headline demands of the Land League. The uproar and agitation in the countryside did not abate immediately. Parnell was imprisoned for a while before a compromise was reached with Gladstone. By then, the whole country was shocked by the vicious Phoenix Park Murders of May 1882, which brought the deaths of the newly-appointed Chief Secretary (the London cabinet minister responsible for Ireland) and the Under-Secretary (the head of the Irish civil service).

Gradually, and to Parnell's private relief, the emphasis now turned from agrarian agitation to politics. His aim was to secure the support of one of the mainstream British parties for the cause of Irish home rule. At the election of 1885, the Liberal Party declined to do so, so Parnell advised Irish voters in Britain to vote Conservative. This unorthodox tactic resulted in a hung parliament, with Parnell's party — by now formidably disciplined and whipped under his leadership — holding the balance of power. Gladstone then discovered that he supported home rule after all, and introduced the first Home Rule Bill (1886), which split his party and was defeated. But Parnell had achieved a political miracle: one of the two great parties was now committed to Irish home rule. Surely the pendulum of parliamentary politics would deliver the goods in time. What had been unthinkable a few years earlier was now one of the central questions in British public life. Parnell was a god in Ireland.

And like a god, he fell. When his affair with Katharine O'Shea, wife of one of his (most useless) MPs, was discovered he was disowned by Gladstone's Liberals — the party was prone to fits of what was called the 'nonconformist conscience'. Gladstone was now faced with either sacrificing Parnell or losing the leadership of Liberalism. He presented the Nationalists with a hideous dilemma. They could have Parnell or the Liberal alliance but not both.

The party split on 15 December 1890. The majority chose the Liberals. Parnell attempted to reconstruct his political fortunes in a series of three bitterly fought by-election campaigns in Ireland over the following year, all of which he lost. The Irish Catholic hierarchy, determined not to be out-moralised by a crowd of English Protestants, turned against him. The Split was a savage business, with passions inflamed beyond reason on both sides. It darkened Irish nationalist life for a generation.

Parnell's frenzied by-election campaigns killed him. Never robust, he was drenched to the skin while addressing a meeting in Creggs, Co. Roscommon and caught a chill which developed into pneumonia. He dragged himself back to Brighton, where he lived with Katharine, and died there on 6 October 1891. His remains were returned to Dublin, where his funeral attracted over 100,000 mourners. He is buried in the most impressive grave in Ireland, in Glasnevin cemetery under a single boulder of Wicklow granite bearing the simple legend PARNELL.

ROBINSON & CLEAVER

The department store is one of the nineteenth century's most enduring legacies. It was an evolutionary, rather than a revolutionary, development. It evolved from bazaars and other markets and from shops where a range of goods were carried under one roof, but the key decade of consolidation was the 1850s, which saw the opening of A. T. Stewart's Marble Palace (1851), New York's first monster store, soon to be followed by Macy's. In Paris, the *grands magasins* were facilitated by the construction of Baron Hausmann's series of enormous radial boulevards. London followed suit, department stores often forming organically by consolidation of existing retail outlets. The first custom-built department store in London only dates from 1877. Nor was it just a capital city phenomenon: as early as 1855, Wylie & Lockhead's store in Glasgow was the first in the United Kingdom to install a lift. And this innovation in Glasgow was telling, for Glasgow was a city transformed by the industrial revolution.

The industrial revolution hardly affected the three southern provinces of Ireland but it had a profound effect in Ulster. The term itself refers to a complex series of economic advances that began in Britain from the 1780s onwards and spread gradually and unevenly through Western Europe in the nineteenth century. The key developments were the harnessing of steam power, the accelerated development of coal and iron mining, the move from domestic piece work by individual craftsmen to factory production by armies of semi-skilled and unskilled workers. This development meant the growth of industrial cities and a surge of population from the countryside to the towns.

In Britain, the industrial revolution was mainly focused in the midlands, north and west. Ireland, with its lack of iron and coal, seemed unpromising territory. But the exception proved to be in eastern Ulster, where the centralisation of the linen bleaching industry in Belfast marked the first stage in the industrialisation of the province and the beginning of Belfast's phenomenal nineteenth-century expansion. Its population in 1808 was about 25,000; in 1901, it was almost 350,000.

In 1828, the York Street linen mill was established. An enormous premises by the industrial standards of the times, it became the focus of Belfast's pre-eminence as a centre of the international linen trade. By 1850, there were sixty-two such mills in Belfast alone. The need to import coal and flax — because the industry had expanded beyond the ability of local resources to supply the mills — meant the development of Belfast port. From this, there grew the shipbuilding industry which was the city's pride in the late Victorian and Edwardian eras.

In 1858 Edward Harland bought a small shipyard in Belfast Lough. Three years later, he went into partnership with Gustav Wilhelm Wolff. Harland & Wolff was to become one of the giants of British shipbuilding: it built the most famous ship ever to sail and sink, the *Titanic*, in 1912. A smaller yard, that of Workman Clark ('the wee yard'), was established on the Lagan in 1880 where it flourished until the Great War before finally closing in 1935.

It was not just linen and ships. The Belfast region produced other textiles, tobacco products, engineering and other commodities typical of the new industrial age. In effect, Ulster east of the Bann became part of the economy of north-west Britain. Its fortunes could hardly have made a greater contrast with the agricultural provinces to the south, reeling from the effects of the Famine. The leaders of industry in Ulster were almost all Protestants: their identification with their co-religionists in Britain was augmented by common economic and material interests. Ulster was becoming more different, not less.

And all this produced a prosperous and confident middle class, one of the essential elements for fixed-place retailing and for department stores. Other essentials included transport links to the city from the growing suburbs, provided by the new trams and buses, and efficient wholesale distribution systems facilitated by the railways.

Donegall Square in the centre of Belfast is dominated by the City Hall, standing on the site of the old White Linen Hall (see chapter 24). The square wraps round it on all four sides. Of the buildings on the square itself, two of the most distinctive and distinguished are the Ocean Building and the former Royal Irish Linen Warehouse, otherwise named for its founding partners, Robinson & Cleaver. Both buildings were designed by the same architects, Young and Mackenzie. None the less, the styles are quite dissimilar. The Ocean Building is solid red sandstone Gothic revival with a hint of Scots baronial but Robinson & Cleaver was altogether different: a light, playful, almost *jugendstil* design, heavily ornamented on the exterior and containing a magnificent central staircase within. It was the grandest department store in the city. It also established branches in Britain, as did its nearest Belfast rival, Anderson & McAuley. R&C had a store in Regent Street in London.

The Belfast building was started in 1886 — the year of the home rule bother — and opened for business two years later. From the start, it was the pre-eminent city centre store for the new-rich bourgeoisie. As its official name suggested, Irish linen was its principal stock-in-trade and it exported linen products all over the world. Some estimates reckoned that one-third of all parcels sent overseas from Belfast originated in this one shop.

Its history was like that of the city it adorned. It retained its swagger into the twentieth century, advertising itself in 1921 in these terms: *We are making a Special Show of our New Season's Models in all the latest shapes in Fur Coats, Wraps, Stoles and Collars in Skunk, Skunk Opossum, Beaver, Beaver Coney and Real Moleskin. Animal Ties in White, Black, Grey, and Blue Foxes; also in Mongolian Fox and Blue Wolf. Only the most reliable quality of Furs is stocked.* But by the 1960s its fortunes were on the slide and it closed for good in 1984, in the darkest days of the Troubles when the city centre became a ghost town in the evenings. The grand staircase was flogged off and the building now houses chain retailers of minimum distinction and maximum ubiquity, together with anonymous office functionaries.

RED BRICK

Nothing will shake the generalisation that Dublin is a Georgian city. The Georgian era made the city and the Georgian building style persisted long into the Victorian era, certainly past 1850. Nevertheless, the city can claim to be as much a Victorian creation as a Georgian one. For this, we can thank the spread of the suburbs.

The suburbs had hardly existed in 1800 when almost the entire population was contained within the ring of the two canals. The suburban population was barely 30,000 in 1831. Then came the railway, which encouraged coastal suburban development on the south side. Blackrock and Kingstown (Dún Laoghaire) slowly began to assume their modern suburban status. Following the Great Famine, the city swelled with wretchedly poor people fleeing from the stricken countryside. This in turn accelerated the flight of the middle classes to the nine new townships.

The townships were independent local authority areas, complete with their own town halls, beyond the reach of Dublin Corporation, whose remit stopped at the canals. They were Rathmines & Rathgar, Pembroke, Blackrock, Kingstown, Dalkey, Killiney, Kilmainham, Drumcondra and Clontarf. The incentive to develop them was driven by a number of factors. The Municipal Corporations Act of 1840 was one. It made the Corporation more representative and less oligarchic. In place of the old series of nominating bodies, all of them exclusively Protestant, the Corporation was now elected by all rate-paying property owners. The measure had been part of a deal made between the Whig government in London and Daniel O'Connell. As a result of this measure, O'Connell became lord mayor of the city in the following year, the first Catholic to hold the office since 1688.

Another was Protestant anxiety. O'Connell's mayoralty was an ill omen for a professional class that was still disproportionately Protestant and that feared a Catholic-dominated Corporation. Added to this was the knowledge that rates — local taxation to fund services — would be lower in the townships than in the city, whose need for cash to address its sundry infrastructural shortcomings would ensure that Corporation rates would be relatively high. It was an article of faith among the township developers that the Corporation was wasteful and spendthrift. In sum, the flight of the well-to-do from the city robbed it of its leading citizens, who now suited themselves in the self-governing suburban townships while turning their backs on the increasing squalor behind them, thus accomplishing a self-fulfilling prophecy.

The division of the classes is the big theme of Victorian Dublin. The poor remained in a decaying, hideously overcrowded centre, many living in conditions of deprivation without parallel in northern Europe. The moneyed middle classes — ever more the social leaders of the city now that the flight of the old aristocracy was almost complete — moved to the townships, but worked, shopped and enjoyed concerts and theatres in the city to which they otherwise made no material contribution. As the city housing situation, especially in the tenements, went from bad to worse, with no clear plan for wholesale slum clearance, the suburbs witnessed a dramatic expansion with the development of delightful red-brick areas like Ranelagh and Ballsbridge. Outlying villages were now swallowed up by the new developments, and the overall effect of this expansion was the creation of a stark binary class division. The continuing decay of the city and the development of lush suburbs were two sides of the one coin.

By 1891, the city population was just over 245,000 but that of the suburbs outside the Corporation area was already past 100,000. Those who could get out of town got out.

Having got out, of course, they needed to get back in for work and pleasure. In this regard, the development of the tramway system was crucial. The first commercial tram ran in Dublin in 1872, on a route from the city to Rathmines. The tramway system spread rapidly, soon overwhelming the primitive omnibus network that had preceded it. In 1891, the three existing companies were consolidated as the Dublin United Tramway Company and the DUTC ran the city's first electric tram in 1896. The DUTC survived until 1945, bequeathing its much-loved 'flying snail' logo to its unloved successor CIÉ.

Complementing access to and from the suburbs was the suburban railway system. Lines operated by the principal mainline companies were gradually studded with suburban halts to serve commuters' needs. The series of southside stations along the Dublin South Eastern line to Wexford still form the backbone of the modern DART service. For example, Sydney Parade in the heart of the Pembroke township was opened as a station in 1852, having previously been a halt.

The reformed Dublin Corporation performed prodigies, despite the cynical flight of the rich. Regulatory functions which had previously been chaotically dispersed among individual parishes and voluntary bodies were now subject to greater central control. The most impressive results were seen in areas like sanitation and public health, where the second half of the century brought major advances. The first medical health officer for the city was appointed in 1874 (Charles Cameron, who made old bones and died in office in 1920). A huge step forward took place with the completion of the Vartry waterworks in 1871. For the first time, it provided the city with a pure water supply at high pressure and was the envy of other, richer cities in Britain and abroad.

The chief promoter of this initiative was the chairman of the waterworks committee, Sir John Gray, whose statue deservedly stands in O'Connell Street. The Vartry's retaining dam held 11 million cubic metres, which then flowed through a 4km long tunnel to a large open service reservoir at Stillorgan before delivering up to 85,000 cubic metres daily to the city.

Hand in hand with this major advance in the city's infrastructure went the development of domestic plumbing systems and the city's sewer system. A Royal Commission on the Sewerage and Drainage of Dublin reported in 1880. It built on a sewerage system that had been begun in 1870 and was to develop into the Main Drainage Scheme in 1892, not reaching its full extent until 1906.

No wonder the rates were high in the city. None of this came cheap. Rathmines township, almost manic in its suspicion of the Corporation, opted out of the Vartry water scheme on grounds of cost, attempting instead to draw potable water from the Grand Canal. Only in 1888 did it admit defeat. Likewise, Rathmines and Pembroke dragged their feet for more than twenty years — again, on grounds of cost — before connecting themselves to the main drainage scheme.

Still, the townships did live up to their promise. Their pleasant and beautiful suburbs are some of Dublin's most attractive modern addresses. The final move from neo-Georgian to Victorian red brick came around the mid-century. In Pembroke, for instance, which was finally incorporated as a township in 1863, Waterloo Road and Upper Leeson Street were developed in imitation Georgian in the 1840s. But as areas adjacent were created — Clyde Road, Raglan Road and Morehampton Road—red brick came to assert itself beyond any challenge. Indeed, a walk southward along Morehampton Road reveals quite starkly where mock-Georgian ends and Victorian red brick begins.

The independent townships were eventually re-incorporated into the city. The northside ones, Drumcondra and Clontarf, lost their independence in 1900 and the rest — with the exception of Kingstown/Dún Laoghaire — in 1929.

PEARSE'S COTTAGE

In 1893, the Gaelic League was formed. The founder was Eoin Mac Néill, an historian of early and medieval Ireland. The first president was Douglas Hyde, the son of a Church of Ireland rector from Co. Roscommon. A scholar and linguist, he had delivered a lecture in 1892 under the title 'The Necessity for De-anglicising the Irish People', in which he called for an arrest in the decline of the Irish language and deplored the advance of what he regarded as a vulgar, English commercial culture.

The new organisation established itself quickly. It had as its aim the revival of Irish as the common vernacular. It conducted language classes. It published stories, plays and a newspaper, *An Claidheamh Soluis* (The Sword of Light). It opposed a campaign led by Mahaffy, the Provost of Trinity College Dublin, to have the language removed from the Intermediate school syllabus. It established language teacher training colleges. By 1908, there were 600 branches of the League around the country.

The Gaelic League successfully revived the Young Irelanders' idea that cultural and linguistic autonomy was a good thing, and was part of a greater national revival. Hyde naïvely thought that the language was a non-political issue on which people of all religious and social backgrounds could meet without rancour. The League was indeed non-political for the first twenty-two years of its life. But its implied purpose was clear: the re-Gaelicisation of Ireland. That was a purpose that could not be kept innocent of politics forever, not in a country like Ireland. In some ways, it was a very Victorian phenomenon, appealing to the same kind of medieval nostalgia that animated the pre-Raphaelites and the arts and crafts movement in England.

Patrick Pearse was born in 1879 in Dublin, the son of an Irish mother and an English father. James Pearse was an ecclesiastical stone carver, a trade for which there was much demand in Ireland in the second half of the nineteenth century. A Christian Brothers education introduced the younger Pearse to the Irish language at the age of fourteen. He was less impressed by the rest of his education: the Christian brothers focused on educating lower-middle-class boys for employment as clerks and civil servants and in the minor professions. Theirs was a utilitarian, Gradgrind kind of teaching that Pearse came to loathe. When, in later life, he opened his own school, it was to espouse an educational philosophy remote from and vastly more enlightened than that of the Brothers.

Pearse joined the Gaelic League in 1896, as his schooldays were ending but before he went to university. Within two years, he had made a sufficient mark to be co-opted to its executive committee, bringing him into close contact with people influential in the language revival movement. He was not yet twenty. He was already teaching Irish in his old school and now began to give classes in the Royal University, where he failed to impress his contemporary, James Joyce. The novelist thought the Irish teacher a bore, whose technique of promoting Irish by denigrating English he deplored. For instance, Pearse offered the view that 'thunder' was a most inadequate word: it was a favourite of Joyce's (despite his chronic fear of thunderstorms).

Pearse first visited the Connemara Gaeltacht in 1898, making his way to the Aran Islands. Thus began a lifelong idealisation of the western peasant, something not unique to him and which was to have a long cultural afterlife. All the time, his command of colloquial and quotidian Irish was improving. In March 1903, he was appointed editor of *An Claidheamh Soluis*. It was also in the spring of 1903 that he first came to Ros Muc in the south Connemara Gaeltacht as an examiner for the Gaelic League. He fell in love with the place and looked around for a site where he could have a summer cottage built for himself.

He bought a site and the two-bedroomed cottage was duly built. It became a place of retreat for Pearse, although he was notoriously slow to pay the bills he incurred in building it. It is thought that there were still bills unpaid at his death in 1916. It was here that he began to compose the oration that he delivered over the grave of the old Fenian Jeremiah O'Donovan Rossa in 1915, one of the finest and most resonating pieces of oratory in Irish history.

Pearse went on to found a school in Dublin, St Enda's, in which he applied his liberal educational theories and promoted his Irish-Ireland linguistic and cultural agenda. There were unpaid bills here too: Pearse was bad with money. He gradually moved from cultural to political nationalism, joined the IRB and was one of the key members of the military council — a self-appointed group within the IRB that organised the rising of 1916. He was formally commander-in-chief of the Irish Volunteers, president of the Provisional Government of the Republic that was declared on the steps of the GPO in Dublin on that Easter Monday, and a signatory of the Proclamation of the Republic. It was he who, at the end of Easter Week, formally surrendered to the British. He was executed on 3 May.

Pearse's cottage became a place of pilgrimage. It also became a locus of myth. Pearse was an emotional man, better with imaginative imagery than with rational calculation. He was not alone in idealising the Irish-speaking peasants and smallholders of the west, but he seemed to stand as a symbol for all who did. And many did. The image of the anti-modern virtuous peasant, uncorrupted by English decadence and urban frivolity, became for a time a prevailing fetish in newly independent Ireland. Similar enthusiasms in contemporary Europe were invariably associated with fascist and reactionary movements.

It suited both church and state in nationalist Ireland to propose a *cordon sanitaire* against modernity. In the church's case, it meant a docile, unquestioning laity. For the state, independence meant a withdrawal from the world rather than an engagement with it. Economic autarky, censorship, wartime neutrality, an emphasis on agriculture rather than on industrial development, an education system that scandalously neglected the sciences in an age of scientific wonders: sometimes the new Ireland seemed very old indeed.

MECHANICS'
INSTITUTE

By injecting a strong cultural element into the national mix, the Gaelic League was part of a larger movement that developed from the 1890s onwards. What is commonly called the Irish Literary Revival was the work of a remarkable generation of writers and intellectuals. It is often represented as a reaction to the sordid politics of the Parnell split and a search for a more honourable and positive means of expressing national sentiment. Certainly, W.B. Yeats thought so. Many years later, when making his acceptance speech in Stockholm upon winning the Nobel Prize for Literature he declared unambiguously:

> The modern literature of Ireland, and indeed all that stir of thought which prepared for the Anglo-Irish war, began when Parnell fell from power in 1891. A disillusioned and embittered Ireland turned away from parliamentary politics; an event was conceived and the race began, as I think, to be troubled by that event's long gestation.

The literary revival — indeed the whole cultural revival of which it was the most distinguished part — drew inspiration from the Young Ireland poets associated with *The Nation* as well as from the work of antiquarians and Celtic scholars in Ireland and on the continent. Like all such movements, it required a central figure. It found it in Yeats.

Yeats was not simply a poet of genius but also a very considerable man of action. He was, with Lady Gregory, the prime mover behind the establishment of Ireland's national theatre, the Abbey, which established itself in the old Mechanics' Institute in Abbey Street, Dublin, in 1904. The Institute was part of a movement that started in Great Britain in the early nineteenth century to provide adult education for the working class. By 1904, when the Abbey bought it, it was variously a venue for Irish-language classes, a music hall and the city morgue.

Yeats was fascinated by mysticism and eastern religion and managed to translate both to a Celtic locale. He shared this enthusiasm with many leading figures in the movement, most notably the remarkable George Russell (AE). It was also, to a remarkable degree for a movement of its kind, Protestant. Yeats, Russell and Lady Gregory, the patron and *éminence grise* of the movement, were all Protestants. So were Synge and O'Casey, its two great dramatists, and many of its minor figures. It has been speculated that they represented an enlightened Protestant vanguard, aware that the game was up for the old order with the disestablishment of the Church of Ireland and the end of the estate system, and anxious to find a role and make a stamp on the new Ireland.

The Gaelic League and the literary revival overlapped in places and shared a common sensibility. Both were anti-utilitarian and romantic. This brought both movements, but especially the literary revival, onto a collision course with the very utilitarian Catholic middle class. This group was the social backbone of quotidian nationalist society. It had little interest in mystic speculation — other than the Catholic devotional kind, which wasn't what Yeats and the others had in mind at all — although its national pride was flattered by the dramatic representation of Irish heroic myths. Yeats's play *Cathleen Ni Houlihan*, first given in Dublin in 1902, was a thinly disguised call to arms against England and famously gave the poet qualms of conscience in later years.

Yeats was many things, including a Fenian sympathiser (perhaps even an actual Fenian for a while), but was consistent in his distaste for the middle class. His thoroughly reactionary dream of a union of aristocrats and peasants ranged against the philistine bourgeoisie left no place for the very people who were inheriting the new nationalist world that was forming all about him. The farmers, shopkeepers, clerks and others of this sort who had been the backbone of Parnell's party had other voices to articulate their concerns and prejudices: voices like those of the brilliantly waspish lawyer and parliamentarian Tim Healy — the most eloquently vituperative of the anti-Parnellites — and D.P. Moran, a journalist with a supreme talent for abuse. His journal, *The Leader*, founded in 1900, was a scabrously entertaining cocktail of lower–middle–class nationalist prejudice directed against Protestants, intellectuals, the English, the rich, nationalists like Arthur Griffith of whom Moran did not approve, and anything and anyone that encouraged the editor's ire. Moran was a bottomless pit of acid.

Yeats's world and Moran's collided in 1907 when Synge's *Playboy of the Western World* opened at the Abbey. Patriotic plays were one thing. The gritty realism of Synge was another. The *Playboy* is set in Co. Mayo and the peasant cast is presented, in part at least, as ignorant, credulous and superstitious. This was deeply offensive to a nationalist audience, which saw only stage-Irish caricature. They also shared the prissy puritanism of the age, so that when a reference was made to a 'shift' — a lady's undergarment or slip — it was the trigger for an already shocked and tense audience to riot.

The *Playboy* riot was not simply a contest between art and philistinism, although this was naturally the myth that Yeats made of it. It was a collision of different mental worlds. Ironically, both were attempting a definition of Irishness that was transforming. For the utilitarian middle class, virtue meant material progress, piety, respectability and movement towards home rule. Indeed, if you subtract the political element, the nationalist middle class had aspirations very similar to their counterparts in the rest of the United Kingdom. After the trauma of the Famine, less than a lifetime before, the advance in material fortunes was a source of pride. Synge's peasants seemed like some sort of pre-Famine horror, drawn by a condescending Protestant in a theatre run by Protestants.

For Yeats and Synge, the autonomy of great art and its fidelity to reality was the supreme virtue. Part of the problem for the audience was precisely that Synge was not drawing stage-Irish characters: they were all too real. Synge had spent many nights in western cottages, listening and noting the vocabulary, syntax and utterances of western peasants. It was his fidelity in reproducing their speech — these people who were now a social embarrassment to the new petit bourgeoisie — that was troubling. Set in the context of a powerful psychological drama, a truly stirring work of art, the tension proved too great.

That tension was caused by a gap between politics and culture in nationalist Ireland that nothing could bridge in the early twentieth century. Nationalist politics had focused on the material, most obviously on the land question. Its organisational methods were borrowed from Tammany Hall and were not for the squeamish. It was hand in glove with the Catholic clergy. It was careful and calculating. The cultural revival occurred after O'Connell and Parnell had set the material template for nationalism. It now attempted to overlay a cultural template and to furnish nationalism with myths and symbols. In this, it had considerable success but its sensibility was always at an oblique angle to the utilitarianism of the political and social mainstream. Unlike many other European nationalisms, where the culture came first and the politics second, in Ireland it was the other way round. In the end, as Yeats would discover, the politics would crush the culture, demanding of it a role subservient to the wishes and prejudices of the new dominant class. Nationalism cannibalised the cultural revival for those titbits it could digest. It rejected the rest.

MARKET SQUARE, THURLES

MARKET SQUARE, THURLES. 8648. W.L.

The Easter Rising of 1916 is often represented as a foundation event. It was not. Irish nationalism was much older than 1916. Rather, the rising was a transformative event, for it raised the stakes in nationalist Ireland's demands. Previously, home rule within the United Kingdom had been the mainstream aspiration. Now, after the executions of the leaders and the threat of conscription towards the end of World War I plus the triumph of Sinn Féin and the annihilation of the old Irish party in the 1918 general election, the demand was for outright independence: for an Irish republic. The rising was the indispensable condition for this change.

The British had blamed Sinn Féin for the rising, although it had exactly nothing to do with it. The confusion arose because Sinn Féin had become a shorthand for every kind of advanced nationalism. After the rising, it was decided that if the cap seemed to fit, nationalists would wear it. The party was reconstituted under the leadership of Éamon de Valera, for whom Arthur Griffith — founder of the original party twelve years earlier — stood aside. Its constitution stated that 'Sinn Féin aims at securing the international recognition of Ireland as an independent Irish Republic' before adding that 'having achieved that status, the Irish people may by referendum freely choose their own form of government'.

This piece of semantic ambiguity was a formula proposed by de Valera, the first public evidence of his serpentine mind. The fact was that Sinn Féin was not uniformly republican, although it was certainly more 'advanced' than the Irish Party, and the possibility needed to be left open that when the Irish people were finally offered their choice, they might choose something other than the republic.

Sinn Féin swept all before it in the general election of December 1918. The Irish Party was wiped out. The new party, true to its pledge, refused to take its seats at Westminster and instead constituted itself as Dáil Éireann, the assembly of the Irish. It met for the first time on 21 January 1919. On the same day, two Catholic policemen were shot dead at Soloheadbeg, Co. Tipperary. This is generally accepted as the first action in the War of Independence, a sporadic series of local ambush battles in certain counties (much depended on the bellicosity and initiative of local commanders) that sputtered in 1919, burst into flame in 1920 and was finally ended by the Truce of July 1921. There followed a drawn-out set of negotiations in London, culminating in the Anglo-Irish Treaty of December 1921 which established the Irish Free State a year later. By then, the island had been partitioned (see chapter 40).

The Irish Republican Army (IRA), as the Volunteers were now styled, was an army nominally under the civilian control of the Dáil but in reality engaged in semi-autonomous local operations. The War of Independence was focused on Munster, and especially on the counties of Tipperary and Cork. It was, first and foremost, an assault on the front line of the British administration in Ireland: the police, in the form of the Royal Irish Constabulary and the Dublin Metropolitan Police. The RIC was the eyes and ears of the state in the countryside; the G Division of the DMP was the intelligence branch of the Dublin force.

At local level, IRA commanders had been harassing the RIC for some time before the Dáil formally passed a motion authorising a boycott of the force in April 1919. In this, they were bowing to reality: the motion came three months after Soloheadbeg, which had occurred without any civilian authority and was triggered by military impatience with political foot-dragging. Further IRA actions had followed in the meantime. Gradually, attacks on the RIC increased during 1919. In response, remote barracks were evacuated. Then, in 1920, the pressure was ramped up. The numbers of attacks increased dramatically, forcing the closure of more and more barracks and securing the capture of much-needed arms for the IRA.

This provoked a crisis in the British administration, for the very sinews of their rule were being compromised. At Easter 1920, over 300 RIC barracks and twenty tax offices were attacked and burned. The British response was to fill the gap with two paramilitary forces made up for the most part of demobbed troops from the Western Front, a police auxiliary force (the Auxiliaries) and a second group known then and ever after as the Black and Tans (because their temporary uniforms reminded people of the hunting pinks of the famous Co. Limerick hunt, the Scarteen Black & Tans).

As potent as all this mayhem in the countryside was Michael Collins' campaign in Dublin. His 'squad' — hand-picked killers — assassinated members of the G division of the DMP and members of British Intelligence, most famously on the morning of Sunday 21 November 1920, when fourteen British agents were killed in their beds. In reprisal, the Black and Tans killed twelve spectators at a football match in Croke Park that afternoon.

In all this catalogue of ambush and reprisal, one of the first senior policemen to die had been RIC Detective Inspector Hunt, and the circumstances of his death tells us much about the disturbed state of nationalist Ireland in those years. On 23 June 1919, in the early days of the conflict, Hunt was shot dead in cold blood and in broad daylight here in the Market Square in Thurles. The IRA man who fired the fatal shot was called Jim Stapleton. Neither he nor any of the other attackers wore any disguise. No one testified against them, and it is too easy to put this down to intimidation — although this was always a factor with the IRA, both then and later. But one witness recalled, 'The crowd jeered, and there were cries of "Up the Republic". There was not the least sympathy for the unfortunate man. Public bodies did not pass a resolution. Scarcely a blind was drawn on the day of the funeral.'

This happened *before* the arrival of the Auxiliaries and the Black and Tans; before the murders by crown forces of the mayors of Cork and Limerick; before the death by hunger strike of another mayor of Cork, Terence MacSwiney; before Bloody Sunday. Nationalist Ireland had withdrawn its consent to be governed by the British, whose rule was no longer legitimate there. The quickening of nationalist ambition following 1916 had reached the point where the greatest possible degree of separation from the United Kingdom was now the demand. And people were prepared to look the other way when daylight murder was committed in support of that demand, not because they were heartless brutes but because their loyalty was finally withdrawn from the British connection — to the extent that it had ever been committed to it — and given to something at once older and newer.

D/I Hunt died practically at the door of the hotel where the GAA had been founded in 1884 and about a mile from where Tom Semple hurled for the Blues up in the Sportsfield (see chapter 41).

DUBLIN TENEMENTS

MICHAEL'S LANE, DUBLIN. 1888. W.L.

In 1936, Robert Collis wrote as follows to the *Irish Press*:

Dubliners are wont to describe their city affectionately as 'an old lady'. When visitors admire her outer garments — the broad streets, the old eighteenth-century houses, Fitzwilliam Square and St Stephen's Green — they smile complacently and feel proud. Lift the hem of her outer silken garment, however, and you will find suppurating ulcers covered by stinking rags, for Dublin has the foulest slums of any town in Europe. Into these 'quaint old eighteenth-century houses' the people are herded and live in conditions of horror.

Collis was a young paediatrician recently returned to his native city after a distinguished early career abroad. He was from a well-known professional family, mainly medical although his father was a solicitor. Indeed his father is mentioned obliquely in *Ulysses* as the principal of the firm of Collis & Ward, which employs Simon Dedalus' despised brother-in-law, Richie Goulding, 'the drunken little cost drawer'.

Dr Collis was addressing a scandal that had gripped Dublin for over a century and that was only then, in the 1930s, being addressed properly. As early as 1805 a heroic clergyman, Rev. James Whitelaw, had produced a report based on his many visitations to the homes of the poor. In stark terms, he described scenes of hopeless poverty and ill-health: incredible overcrowding, with sometimes even single rooms being sub-divided to provide a minimal and miserable living space; the complete absence of any sanitary clearance system; dung heaps — for human and animal waste alike — and rubbish middens in enclosed back yards; open sewers; the noxious or filthy by-products of commercial activities like lime-kilns.

The early-nineteenth-century city was still small, almost wholly contained within the two canals. In this limited space, the population had risen to more than 200,000 people. Even with growing social segregation, wealth and poverty were uncomfortably close. Wealth demanded servants, who could carry infectious diseases from the slums to the homes of the mighty.

The Liberties was an area that had been largely untouched by eighteenth-century splendour. It was here that Whitelaw found the very worst conditions. In 1818, he described 'many large houses, consisting of a number of rooms; each of these rooms is let to separate tenants, who again re-let them to as many individuals as they can contain, each person paying for that portion of the floor which his extended body can occupy'.

The very worst of the public health hazards described so memorably by Whitelaw were alleviated by Victorian public works systems, especially the Vartry water scheme and the sewerage system (see chapter 34). But the problem of overcrowding in wretched tenement buildings persisted. Nearly all of these houses had been built as elegant town houses for the eighteenth-century rich. They had long since fallen into decay, being abandoned by their original owners as Dublin's fortunes declined after the Act of Union, and were now owned by rentiers whose principal concern was to squeeze as much income as possible from them, and from the wretched tenants shoe-horned into them.

Some of these slum landlords were members of Dublin Corporation, which gave the city authorities minimal incentive to tackle the scandal of the slums. Moreover, the limited local government franchise meant that well-to-do business and property interests could exercise a disproportionate influence on the Corporation.

As with the Famine, ideology also played its part. The rights of property were asserted with religious conviction: private property was sacrosanct because it represented the surest barrier to the tyranny of the state by securing the autonomy of free individuals. This was neither a stupid nor a wicked view, but its elevation into a sort of fetish in Victorian times frustrated all efforts to involve public bodies and public money in addressing slum clearance. People close to the problem, like Sir Charles Cameron, the long-serving Medical Officer of Health for the city, had persistently called for the direct involvement of public agencies, including the state itself, but this remained a taboo until the end of British rule.

Nor was it just a British taboo. Most leading nationalists shared this belief in the sanctity of private property. Universal male suffrage did not arrive until 1918. Prior to that date, and despite a number of Reform Acts that widened the franchise, only 5.6 million out of a total British population of 36 million had the vote. It was effectively confined to rate-paying property owners and the more substantial tenants. Women, like the poor, were excluded entirely. This meant that the political class came from and appealed to the prosperous minority.

Moreover, the politicians looked to their own interests. William Field, a Dublin Parnellite MP from 1892 until 1918, was also chairman of the Victuallers' Association and the Cattle Traders' Association. These meat trade lobbies were active in opposing all attempts by public health bodies to regulate their trade. Diseased meat was sold to the poor. In 1870 alone, the public health authorities seized 400,000 lbs of diseased meat intended for sale. Indeed, the increasing activity of these authorities in the second half of the nineteenth century is one of the reasons Field and others established their trade associations, and used their considerable political muscle to frustrate all attempts at regulation and supervision of their activities. Field was not a wicked man, just a man of his times.

Nor were the meat interests alone in this. Milk suppliers regularly adulterated their product with water, often drawn from contaminated sources like the canals. Brewers watered their beer but then added narcotic chemicals to give it the required kick. All these mercantile interests shared a belief in the sacred inviolability of private property — thus their hostility to regulation — and simply did not have the mental and imaginative resources to address the slum problem.

Private Victorian initiatives such as the Dublin Artisans' Dwelling Company and the Guinness Trust, while successful in themselves, left the greater part of the problem untouched. It was not until the new state took a direct hand in the matter in the 1920s and 1930s that real progress started to be made. The beautifully laid-out Marino estate on the north side was a product of the 1920s. On the south side, Crumlin, bigger than Marino and less successful visually and architecturally, was none the less a blessing for families who had hitherto faced nothing other than exorbitant rents in squalid city centre tenements. Nearby, Drimnagh was also developed as a public housing estate in a similar fashion, as were Cabra and Finglas on the north side. This all meant the commitment of public funds on a lavish scale, an achievement all the more meritorious for the fact that the state was poor.

The effect was that the twentieth century and an independent government managed to resolve the biggest social problem that had defeated the nineteenth-century British administration. Other forces helped, not least Catholic lay organisations like the Legion of Mary, whose Marian ardour was offended by the widespread prostitution in the city and which campaigned successfully to close the Monto town. They saw the overcrowded slums as a breeding ground for vice: a by-product of their zeal was the increased political pressure which the Catholic church — by now in a position of uncontested moral authority in the country — could bring to bear on government.

39

MARIAN SHRINE, LIBERTIES 1929

This modest and unremarkable Marian shrine was erected in the heart of Dublin's Liberties, one of the inner city's most cohesive working-class communities, to mark the centenary of Catholic Emancipation. In its understated way, it was a gesture as telling as the triumphalist Eucharistic Congress that took place in the city three years later.

The new state was conspicuously Catholic and made little attempt to conceal it. Republican theory was nominally non-sectarian, with endless rather desperate appeals to the several Protestant icons in the nationalist Pantheon, all of whom unfortunately shared the disability of having been unrepresentative of their own confessional community. Less sophisticated people felt no such need to pretend that the new Ireland was anything other than a Catholic country.

The Catholic church liked the idea of Ireland as a kind of spiritual quarantine from which the excesses of secular modernity were excluded. The ultramontane church bequeathed by Cardinal Cullen in the nineteenth century was authoritarian, dogmatic and — approaching the middle years of the twentieth century — at the height of its influence and prestige. Its moral writ ran with irresistible force.

It was quite a thing to be a Catholic bishop in Ireland in the mid-twentieth century. It was a guarantee of immense deference and prestige. Catholic Ireland, it seemed, was the last vibrant corner of the Victorian world. Religious observance and devotion were nearly universal. Almost every Catholic went to Mass each Sunday; abstention was a social scandal. There were sodalities, public processions, devotions such as benediction and the forty hours, missions and retreats, and an overwhelming Marian cult. There were priests everywhere. Churches were full to overflowing. Catholic pamphlets and tracts and devotional books sold strongly. There was little or no public criticism of the Church or any tradition of anti-clericalism. It was said by some that the people were not priest-ridden, rather that the priests were people-ridden, so ubiquitous was the spirit of submissive orthodoxy.

When the coalition government of 1948–51 — the first non-de Valera administration since 1932 — tried to introduce free medical care for mothers and children under 16, it sparked off a church–state clash which the church won hands down. The sponsoring minister, a left-wing maverick named Noël Browne, was forced to resign. Members of the cabinet wrote to John Charles McQuaid, the archbishop of Dublin and principal opponent of the scheme, in the most fawning and obsequious terms to demonstrate their loyalty. McQuaid's objection was that Catholic social teaching decreed that services such as Browne proposed were the province of the family rather than the state.

Relations with Protestants were cool to frigid. Ecumenism was for the future. For the moment, the church insisted on the primacy of its teaching and held all other Christian groups to be in varying degrees of error. This was not a church that encouraged theological speculation or internal debate.

The Irish Catholic church also had an enormous missionary presence overseas. In every part of the English-speaking world and in most of Africa, Irish priests, nuns and brothers were to be found. By the middle of the century, there were more than 10,000 Irish missionaries scattered around the world, not counting priests of Irish birth who chose to serve overseas. It was an impressive statistic for a country so sparsely populated. The Irish church regarded its missionary outreach as a spiritual analogue to Britain's material empire and all the more honourable for that. The Irish missionaries did not simply spread the faith; they provided teachers and medical personnel in huge numbers.

At home, the entire education system was denominational — this key ambition of the church had been fulfilled promptly in the 1920s on securing independence. The schools were run by priests, nuns and brothers. The latter, in particular, educated generations of lower-middle-class boys who might otherwise have received little or no schooling at all. Still, it was a severely utilitarian type of education for the most part — another Victorian survival. And behind the benign and selfless achievements of generations of clerical teachers lay the dark secret of sexual abuse of minors, in schools, orphanages and penal institutions run for the state by religious orders.

The traditional church was obsessed with sex and the sins of the flesh. These were, in a sense, the only real sins. The deep Puritanism of the church was partly a further manifestation of an antique world in which so-called Victorian values persisted long after they had been subverted elsewhere. But it was also a psychological prop in the whole post-Famine settlement. The need for marriages to be delayed until farms could be inherited; the wretched celibacy of many who had nothing to inherit and therefore nothing to offer a spouse; the extraordinary prestige in which celibate clergy were held: these were social contrivances, designed to stabilise rural society in the post-Famine period. Irish society got the morality it needed. In this as in much else, church and people were one.

STORMONT

The Government of Ireland Act 1920 was, in effect, the fourth attempt to introduce home rule. The bills of 1886 and 1893 had failed. The 1914 act had passed but had been suspended for the duration of World War I and by 1918 it was a dead letter. The 1920 act replaced it, and in the process, provided for the partition of the island.

The Lloyd George government established a cabinet committee to address the Irish situation, chaired by Walter Long, a Wiltshire landowner influential in Tory politics. He had briefly been chief secretary for Ireland and was a vocal and committed unionist partisan. His committee acknowledged two realities: that the southern provinces must be granted home rule and that Ulster must not be coerced into the new autonomous state.

Long's committee recommended partition and the creation of two parliaments, one for the three southern provinces and one for the nine historic counties of Ulster. But Sir James Craig, the hatchet-faced whiskey millionaire who was the great organiser of Ulster unionism, realised that a nine-county option would be too evenly balanced between nationalists and unionists for comfort, and that any nationalist majority would instantly vote for unity with the south. So he lobbied for and secured a line of partition that excluded the three counties of Cavan, Monaghan and Donegal, which had the smallest Protestant populations.

The remaining six counties had a rock-solid Protestant-unionist majority and it was for this community and for them alone that Northern Ireland was created under the 1920 act. The one part of the island that had fought most bitterly against home rule was the only part to get it. The Catholics of Northern Ireland, about 35 per cent of the population, regarded partition as a betrayal that delivered them into the hands of their tribal enemies.

The IRA did its best to strangle Northern Ireland at birth, which was accompanied by an orgy of sectarian violence in the years 1920–22. The war of independence spread north and became entangled with the trauma of partition. The IRA attacked police and the army as in the south; Protestant mobs drove Catholic workers from the Belfast shipyards; the IRA retaliated by burning businesses and big houses in rural Ulster to try to take the pressure off their beleaguered co-religionists in Belfast; the UVF was re-formed as the Ulster Special Constabulary — the notorious B Specials — a viciously partisan Protestant militia; sixty-one people died in Belfast alone in the single month of March 1922.

In essence, the sectarian civil war that had been postponed by the outbreak of the Great War had now broken out in the Ulster cockpit. Inevitably, given the local superiority of Protestant numbers and the fact that they controlled the levers of the state, the Protestants were able to bring a greater terror to bear than the Catholics. There were atrocities committed on both sides: it was not all one-way traffic. But the Protestant traffic was more lethal. Moreover, it polluted its own community, as well as terrorising the Catholic one, by permitting the agents of the newly partitioned statelet literally to get away with murder.

The new state was therefore born on the back of a military victory for the unionists in 1922, something neither side forgot. Nationalists were to be a despised enemy in the eyes of their new rulers. Ulster unionists created a state in their own image and for their own community. From the first, Northern Ireland was obsessed with community security. The police were augmented by the Ulster Special Constabulary (the B Specials), an armed local militia, who were effectively the UVF in another guise. Many were Great War veterans. Few were squeamish about violence, a lack of scruple which was in fairness reciprocated by the IRA. The police and the USC had at their backs the Special Powers Act, originally enacted in 1922 at the height of the IRA war to give the state emergency powers. It was not repealed until 1973. In effect, it gave the Minister of Home Affairs power to rule by decree. In its indifference to civil liberties and the normal constitutional checks and balances, it was unique in the western world.

The physical symbol of the little statelet was the new parliament building opened at Stormont, in solidly Protestant east Belfast, in 1932. It is a fine neo-Grecian pile set on rising ground in pleasant parkland. Never has such an exiguous assembly had a more ostentatious home. At that, it was a pared-down version of an even more megalomaniacal complex which had to be abandoned because of the recession that gripped the whole world following the Wall Street crash of 1929. The architect was Sir Arnold Thornley, who also designed the Port of Liverpool Building. It was clad in Portland stone to give a dazzling white effect when seen from the distant gates as one looked up the hill. During World War II, it was covered in a coating of bitumen and cow dung to camouflage it from German bombers, in which ambition it succeeded but at the cost of permanent discoloration of the stonework.

Northern Ireland was financially beholden to London and unable to formulate any economic policy to deal with the damage done to the local economy in the aftermath of the Wall Street crash. Things were so bad in the early 1930s that the unemployed briefly threw aside their sectarian animosities to form a united front. This moment did not last and 1935 saw the worst sectarian rioting in Belfast since 1922.

World War II brought a temporary revival, as the economy went on a war footing and unemployment was almost eliminated. There was also a generational change in unionism. Craig, the first prime minister of the province, died in 1940 and was succeeded first by John Miller Andrews, who was ousted by a party revolt in 1943. This brought the younger and more energetic Basil Brooke (later to become Lord Brookeborough) to power, a change that did not signify any liberalising of sectarian attitudes. Even the shared privations of the war — Belfast was bombed heavily by the *Luftwaffe* in 1941 and hundreds died — did nothing to lessen communal divisions or the essentially sectarian nature of the partition.

Both sides were caught in a trap with nowhere to go. Unionist gain could only mean nationalist loss and vice versa. The logic of the nationalist position was as bleak. Unable to challenge the existence of the state and incapable of recognising its legitimacy, its politics were condemned to futility. In local government, where there might be a nationalist majority, unionists ensured their continued dominance through a shameless policy of gerrymandering. Derry was the most notable but not the only example of this.

The establishment of the British welfare state after World War II disturbed this pattern. The benefits of the new system — combined with those of the British educational reforms which effectively opened up secondary schooling to all regardless of income or creed — were applied indiscriminately. Some unionist ultras resented what they regarded as the rewarding of treachery, and indeed it was to have devastating consequences for unionism in the late 1960s.

From 1956 to 1962 the IRA conducted a sporadic campaign of bombings, arms raids and ambushes along the border. It was a sad coda to this whole period, a half-hearted effort which seemed to symbolise the enervated state of militant republicanism. There were many minor actions, but most were contained in west Ulster. There was no mass mobilisation of nationalists. Belfast was almost untouched. Brookeborough introduced internment and locked up as many militants as he could find. Interestingly, de Valera did the same in the Republic: no one was going to out-republican him. In all, twelve IRA men and six policemen died in the border campaign. It was such small beer compared to what was to come.

SEMPLE STADIUM

I f the Gaelic League attempted to stay non-political, the other key cultural organisation of the period from the Parnell split to the Easter Rising had no such inhibitions. On the contrary, the Gaelic Athletic Association was a Fenian vehicle from the start. It has also been the most successful popular association in modern Irish history.

It was founded in Thurles, Co. Tipperary, in 1884. Its purpose was to preserve and promote the ancient game of hurling. In addition, it developed a code of football which went on to become the most popular spectator sport in twentieth-century Ireland. For the Fenians, it offered a perfect recruiting vehicle and its politics reflected Fenian radicalism right from the beginning. It was aggressively Parnellite at the time of the split and thereafter was to be found on the left of the nationalist movement on every occasion. It was republican in politics; hugely supportive of the Irish language and of Gaelic culture in general; tacitly Catholic, although not clerical, in its assumptions; and ferociously opposed to the symbols of British rule, not least the police. It imposed a ban on its members playing 'foreign games' — defined as soccer, rugby, hockey and cricket — which lasted until 1971.

In part, it was a reaction against the exclusiveness of other sports. Rugby was focused on elite private schools; cricket had a long association with both army and ascendancy; athletics was administered by a Trinity College elite which discouraged, to put it no more strongly, the participation of the wrong sort of chaps. The GAA was perfect for the people whose faces did not fit. To be fair, this point can easily be exaggerated: there is much local evidence from the late 1880s, when things were still fluid, that GAA clubs were founded by athletes who cheerfully played cricket and association football (soccer). The exclusiveness was not all one way: the ban on foreign games was also a form of exclusion, a kind of recreational tariff wall willed by the Fenian element in the GAA for political-cultural reasons.

At any rate, the GAA became the great popular mobilising force in Irish recreational life. And it did so in a context that applauded exclusion, that insisted on the separateness of Gaelic games and the social life that revolved around them. Matches were played on Sundays, the only free day in the working week, which guaranteed that sabbatarian Protestants were unlikely to participate. The GAA soon spread to every Catholic parish in the country, with a local club often named for a saint or a patriot: thus Naomh (Saint) this-or-that, plus various Emmets, Tones, Sarsfields and so on. There were few named for O'Connell, whose aversion to violence made him *persona non grata* in Fenian eyes.

The codification of sports — a mid-Victorian phenomenon — meant the establishment of uniform rules for a game from a multitude of regional variants. The antecedents of soccer and rugby were local rough-and-tumbles with local rules. The codification of hurling followed a similar path to other sports. The game had been particularly popular in three areas in pre-Famine times: in south Leinster and east Munster; on either side of the middle reaches of the Shannon; and in the Glens of Antrim. The Famine dealt what was nearly a death blow to the game in the first two areas. It was the need to revive hurling that inspired the founders of the GAA.

And revive it they did. But in codifying the game they faced a problem. The game played in the Glens of Antrim was significantly different to the southern game, being closer to Scottish shinty. Modern hurling was, however, codified along the lines of the South Leinster game. Antrim had to adjust accordingly if it was to participate at national level, which it has done with immense commitment but little success.

The early years of the twentieth century established a pattern that has persisted to the present day, with only occasional interruptions. Three counties, all bordering on each other, have dominated the All-Ireland championship: Kilkenny, Tipperary and Cork. Between them, they have won more than 70 per cent of all championships since the first contest in 1887. Of the other counties that have won the championship more than once, only Dublin (last victory in 1938) doesn't have a border with one of the Big Three. Antrim have never won it at all.

Hurling is effectively a regional rather than a truly national sport, in that it is only played seriously in its heartland. That heartland is the flat limestone countryside south of the Dublin–Galway line. In general, once you hit the rising ground and head into hilly areas, it yields to football.

Yet it is thought of as the national game because of its uniqueness and despite its regional bias. In this it is similar to Australian Rules, another regional game unique to its locale. While hurling may not be as popular as Gaelic football — which is played with varying degrees of skill and success everywhere in Ireland — it is still capable of drawing impressive crowds to big championship matches. It is, moreover, a quite magnificent spectacle when well played, a game of astonishing speed, skill, robust courage and elegance.

Sport demands heroes, and Gaelic games are no exception. In addition, it demands spiritual homes: Newmarket, Lord's, Yankee Stadium, Camp Nou. For hurling, hero and home meet in Thurles, where the GAA was founded.

Tom Semple (1879–1943) was the first great hero of Tipperary hurling. A railway worker, he was the talisman of one the greatest of all club teams, the Thurles Blues (later Thurles Sarsfields), who dominated the game in Tipperary in the first decade of the twentieth century. Prior to the emergence of the Blues, hurling in the county had been very much the property of rural parishes like Moycarkey, Tubberadora and Dungourney. Since the rise of the Blues to eminence, the club has consistently been the dominant force in the county game, having won more county championships than any other.

One contemporary writer rhapsodised about Semple as follows:

> Few men playing the game in Ireland today have achieved the fame that the Thurles captain — Tom Semple — has known. As an organiser and a player he deserves a high place in any story of the progress of hurling during the infancy of the twentieth century. Tom is a conspicuous man — there is no chance of mistaking another player for Semple ... in build, Semple is one of the tall, sinewy type, more of a thoroughbred than a hunter, if I may so express myself. He is well over six feet in his 'vamps' and, like most Tipperary men, square cut and hard as nails.

A various man, Semple became a referee, trainer and a respected administrator. He also used his role as a guard on the Dublin–Cork railway line to act as an IRA courier during the war of independence. He was the trainer of the winning Tipperary championship side in 1930 and was a key figure in securing and developing the Thurles Sportsfield. This ground quickly established itself as everyone's favourite hurling venue in the country. It is the spiritual home of the Munster hurling championship and second-biggest GAA ground in the country by capacity. The final of the All-Ireland championship — normally played in Croke Park in Dublin — was staged in Thurles in 1934 and 1984 to mark the golden jubilee and centenary of the GAA.

The Sportsfield was re-developed in the 1960s and again in the 1980s. In 1971, it was renamed Semple Stadium, in honour of the great hurler who was twenty-eight years dead at the time and whose last championship season as a player had been sixty years earlier. It is the best place of all to watch the national game.

STRONG FARMER'S HOUSE

When British reformers and free traders despaired of Ireland's pre-Famine economy, one of their complaints was that Ireland had no yeoman class. The reformers overstated their case. All pre-Famine visitors to Ireland agreed that the very poorest parts of the country were wretched by any comparative standard. But it is important to emphasise regional differences, which were very marked before the Famine and persisted thereafter. Ireland had large areas of subsistence agriculture before the Famine but also a vigorous commercial agriculture as well. The fattening of cattle for export dominated the economies of most eastern counties around Dublin. Munster was a centre of dairying and the export provision trade through Limerick and Cork (see chapter 29). The south-east, with its more favourable climate, was a tillage zone. Ulster, as usual, was different again with linen introducing an element of rural industry that had no comparable parallel further south (see chapter 24).

One piece of key evidence for the presence of a vigorous commercial agriculture is the number of fairs, the markets at which goods and produce are exchanged for cash. As early as the 1770s, there were already 3,000 of them and by the outbreak of the Famine that number had risen to 5,000.

But still, there was a problem of subsistence and sub-division that the Famine solved. The appalling levels of death and emigration fell most heavily upon the landless poor and the cottiers, the people at the bottom of the heap. It also ruined many landlords and changed the Irish rural economy and the balance of forces in the countryside for good.

Farm sizes increased in every county. This was most marked in the west, simply because the problem had been greatest there. One effect of the Famine was to invigorate commercial farming, effectively end sub-division and subsistence where it existed, and to reward those regions and rural economies that had been most prosperous before the calamity. If Ireland had lacked a yeoman class before the Famine, it acquired one after it. The absence of such a class had far less to do with the nature of Irish agriculture than with the system of land tenure.

Before the Famine, relations between landlord and tenant was regarded as a simple matter of contract law, an agreement between two contracting parties. Government interference through legislation in what was regarded as a free transaction between individuals was thought unnecessary and oppressive. The Encumbered Estates Acts of 1848 and 1849, legislative mechanisms whereby debt-ridden estates could be sold off free of encumbrances, subverted that principle. Parliament was now a player, since the law of contract had proved unequal to the task.

There were to be eighteen Irish land acts passed between 1870 and 1903, all intended to equalise the relationship between landlord and tenant by positive discrimination in favour of the latter. Gladstone's act of 1870 was the start of this process, but like many beginnings it fed an appetite rather than satisfying it. In October 1879 the Land League was formed in Co. Mayo by Michael Davitt, the son of an evicted tenant farmer from Co. Mayo. An ex-Fenian with a conviction for gun-running, Davitt was dedicated to the wholesale overthrow of the landlord system.

The founding of the Land League coincided with an agricultural depression and a consequent reduction in agricultural earnings. The threat of eviction loomed for tenants unable to pay their rents. Memories of the Famine only a generation old stiffened the determination to resist, especially in the West where the human devastation had been greatest. Irish-American money provided the means to organise. A loose administrative structure meant that the best organised and most ruthless could dominate the organisation, and that meant Fenians and other advanced nationalists. The demand was simple: peasant proprietorship.

By the autumn of 1880, the land war was in full swing. Across the country — except, significantly, in most of Ulster — agrarian protesters who previously had merely sought rent abatements in view of the recession were now demanding the abolition of the entire landlord system. Rent increases were refused and rents withheld. Evictions were resisted by violence; where they occurred, revenge was taken on landlords either by attacks on themselves or their livestock; murders, burnings and boycotting increased.

The land war escalated into a wholesale attack on the landlords not just for what they were but for what they represented: the British connection. Nationalist politics now cross-pollinated with agrarian demands in a manner unthinkable in O'Connell's day. Critically, Parnell threw his weight behind the Land League for a few vital years. The landlords were portrayed as a British garrison holding Ireland for the crown against the will of the people. The social authority of the ascendancy was fatally wounded. The solidarity of the tenants was now the key agent of social control. To take up a farm from which another had been evicted was to guarantee being boycotted (the word originated in the land war). Land League courts effectively supplanted crown courts in many parts of rural Ireland, foreshadowing the Sinn Féin courts of 1919–21.

Gladstone's second Land Act — that of 1881 — conceded the 'Three Fs': the right of free sale by an outgoing tenant; fixity of tenure to replace ordinary tenancies; and a fixed rent to be determined by land courts. This drew the sting from the land war, although it never completely subsided for the rest of the decade. Parnell then turned from the land question to the politics of home rule and distanced himself from later agrarian agitation. The problem had been alleviated but not resolved.

That did not happen until 1903, when the chief secretary, George Wyndham, introduced the Land Act that has ever since borne his name. Wyndham's Act provided government funds to buy out the Irish landlords and transfer the land to the former tenants, who now became independent proprietors. Thus the independent family farm came to pass. The act resulted from a conference at which all interests had been represented, so it was a consensual piece of legislation. The main principles had been hammered out at this conference of landlords and tenants, in which the former were the guiding spirits. This was remarkable, considering the mayhem in the countryside a mere twenty years earlier. It was a tacit admission from the landlords that the game was up. With the collapse of tenant deference, the tide had been going out on the old Ascendancy.

It was a transformative piece of legislation and a moment of triumph for the former tenants, who were now established as proprietors and the most significant social group in the country, dominating its affairs until the 1960s. They were for the most part conservative, cautious and un-dynamic: what they had acquired they held. The word 'yeoman' never caught on in Ireland. Instead, the most prosperous of the new owner-occupiers were known simply as 'strong farmers' and typically, they lived in houses like the one shown here.

THE COVE OF CORK

This splendid view from the water at Cobh was the last that generations of emigrants saw of Ireland. From the Famine to World War II, more people left the country through this port of departure than through any other. This pretty town, with its commanding cathedral, was also the last port of call for the *Titanic* in 1912.

Cobh was so named in 1922, having been previously called Queenstown following Queen Victoria's visit of 1849. Despite suggestions that Cobh is a restoration of an older Gaelic name (as in Dún Laoghaire/Kingstown), it is simply a gaelicisation of the English word 'cove', which rather understates what the place is. The town in its modern form dates only from the Napoleonic era, when it became a Royal Navy centre. But its real image in the collective Irish memory is its association with the emigrant ship.

The Famine did not precipitate mass emigration from Ireland. But it hugely accelerated a pattern that was already well established. The best estimate of numbers leaving Ireland in the first half of the nineteenth century is at least a million people. In the twenty years after the Famine, that number trebled. The poorest went to England on the shortest and cheapest passage. Those emigrating to America or Australia (other than convicts) were not exactly well-to-do but either had or had been able to raise the greater fare required. Some were funded by 'improving' landlords anxious to clear their estates of supernumerary tenants. These emigrants also required greater fortitude, because of the tyranny of distance. A passage to America — and *a fortiori* to Australia — was for keeps. The chances were that you would never see Ireland again.

The number of Irish-born people living in Britain increased by 75 per cent between 1841 and 1851. Even in 1841, before the Famine, the Irish represented just over 2 per cent of the British population. By 1851, the figure was 3.5 per cent, but the Irish represented 15 per cent of the total increase in the British population in those ten years.

As we have seen, farm sizes increased after the Famine. More importantly, partible inheritance and sub-division stopped. This meant that large families, which were the norm, could no longer accommodate relatives assisting. Inheritance was now from parents — often elderly — to eldest son, now often past his prime. Thus the integrity of the family holding was maintained at all costs, reinforced by the puritan sexual morality of ultramontane Catholicism. Not for the first time, Christ and Caesar were hand in glove: sexual frolics, as practised in pre-Famine days, were now taboo. Ireland was set upon a path of sexual discipline that would last for a century. It is easy to sneer at aspects of this regime from the second decade of the twenty-first century, but it was part of a response to an overwhelming trauma. The Famine was an existential crisis, which generated an unprecedented response.

The emphasis on the integrity of the farm meant that younger sons either had to find work in towns, as clerks or in the retail trades or some such, or emigrate. Likewise the daughters: Ireland was unusual among European countries in the proportion of its nineteenth-century emigrants that was female. As to destination, in the second half of the century, and up to World War I, more than four-fifths of all Irish emigrants went to America. By the middle of the twentieth century, more than four-fifths were going to Britain, that heartbreaking generation of post-World War II emigrants who were forgotten by their homeland.

There was a correlation — elusive in strictly statistical terms, but suggestive — between reduced rates of emigration and increased rates of agrarian crime. In a countryside where tensions between landlord and tenant were growing ever more antagonistic, and were to run out of control in the 1880s, emigration by the more enterprising and ambitious young removed a volatile element from the social equation. When this slackened, as in the mid 1870s, agitation increased. A generation later, the closing of the emigration routes during World War I was a significant factor in advancing the Irish revolution: all those energetic young men who might have been lost to America were trapped at home, restless.

The Irish experience of emigration is indelibly coloured by a collective memory of suffering. The horrors of the Famine-era coffin ships, in which the conditions of passage were unendurable for the weak and the fevered, were no myth. They were real. Nevertheless, a myth was made of them. The coffin ships became the central mental image of Irish emigration, the first one that flashed to mind. The fact that these inhuman conditions were both a product of the disaster and confined to the years of the Famine and its immediate aftermath did not change this. Emigration came to be seen as a tragedy, or at least a great sadness, sundering families forever (although the integrity of the farm demanded that they be sundered) and all having its certain origin in the heartless British response to the Famine. The unfailing support of Irish-America for radical Irish nationalism ever after was a direct product of this sensibility.

The Irish in America had two priceless advantages: the English language and an understanding of political mobilisation learned from O'Connell. These they put to work by dominating the Democratic Party in the big east-coast cities, controlling local wards through family networks and a spoils system. The shorthand for all this was Tammany Hall, after the party's New York City headquarters. Indeed, the Irish abroad in all the English-speaking countries followed a similar pattern of political and industrial mobilisation. Both the trade union movement and the Labour Party in Britain had a significant Irish presence, something even truer in Australia.

The political and constitutional revolution of 1916–22 had almost no effect on patterns of emigration which were determined by social and economic impulses beyond the reach of politics. As we saw, the destinations changed with Britain displacing America as the twentieth century wore on. Irish construction workers — many of them employed in unskilled and semi-skilled jobs outside the reach of the British taxation and welfare system — made an indispensable contribution to post-war reconstruction.

The population of independent Ireland fell relentlessly in every census from 1926 to 1961 (except for a statistically insignificant upward blip in 1951). Embarrassingly, the population of Northern Ireland grew modestly in every census from 1926 onward, even during the Troubles. In the Republic, the 1950s was the nadir of this dismal trend. The population fell by nearly 5 per cent despite a high birth rate and greatly improved infant mortality figures. The reason was simple: over 400,000 people left a country whose total population, at the start of the decade, was less than 3 million. One in eight Irish people could not find a living at home. This was not simply a reproach to Irish nationalism: it was the product of its economics. The economics of protection, import substitution and attempted self-sufficiency — which went back to the original Sinn Féin at the start of the century — finally collapsed. The recovery of the 1960s, modest enough in itself although spectacular when set against the immediate past, was no more than Ireland belatedly joining the international capitalist post-war boom and opening itself up to inward investment and international trade.

The population of the Republic grew by just over 2 per cent between 1961 and 1966 and inaugurated an upward pattern uninterrupted since (except for another insignificant blip in 1991). In 2011, the population was almost 4.6 million. Sixty years earlier, at the lowest point of the post-Famine exodus, it had been 2.96 million. That is an increase of almost 55 per cent in a single lifetime.

That increase has happened despite the renewal of emigration in the depressed 1980s — although subsequently reversed — and again in the post-Celtic Tiger bust. The shadow of Cobh cathedral no longer looms over the modern emigrant but its image is there in the memory.

BUSÁRAS

T here are patterns in things. Independent Ireland in its first forty years of life placed an emphasis on inwardness. The economics of self-sufficiency; the ban on 'foreign games'; the literary censorship and the social control exercised by an authoritarian national church — which is what Catholicism was in all but name — were the product of a common sensibility.

Official Ireland placed premium value on things thought to be distinctively Irish. The three southern provinces that constituted the new state were the only substantial part of the British Isles almost completely untouched by the industrial revolution. It was perhaps inevitable that the governing class in the Free State/Republic should value agriculture over industry, rural over urban, tradition over modernity. All this reflected the social ascendancy of the farmer, that key vocational group in post-Famine Ireland, liberated into ownership of the land since the 1903 act. It was also a way of marking distance and difference: the Importance of Being Not British.

It dovetailed neatly with international Catholicism's official denunciation of 'modernism', defined loosely as the attempt to reconcile church doctrine with post-Enlightenment philosophical developments, the scientific revolution and a theology that placed greater emphasis on reason than on authority. The Irish Catholic church was enthusiastic in its hostility to this modernism, not least because aspects of modernist theology converged on and were influenced by Protestantism.

There were other forms of modernism that had a cold reception in the new Ireland. The modern movement in fine art left the country almost untouched until the establishment of the White Stag Group and the Irish Exhibition of Living Art in the 1940s, a latter-day *salon des refusés* for artists rejected by the annual exhibitions of the Royal Hibernian Academy. Even then, abstraction did not move towards the mainstream until the 1960s.

It is hardly surprising, therefore, that Ireland was barely touched by the international modern style in architecture between the 1920s and the 1960s. When O'Connell Street in Dublin was being re-built after the destruction caused first by the 1916 rising and later by the civil war, it was done in a conservative commercial classicism typical of the first quarter of the new century. Although not adventurous, it gave Lower O'Connell Street, in particular, a pleasing and restrained architectural coherence. The old Georgian classicism was gone for good and the city architects — C.J. McCarthy and his successor, the wonderfully named Horace Tennyson O'Rourke — resisted any temptation to restore it as pastiche. In Upper O'Connell Street, the Gresham Hotel (1927) was designed by the English architect Robert Atkinson. Its discreet neo-classicism, with just a hint of Egyptian decorative themes then in vogue, is particularly successful. But it was safe. Modern architecture, on the other hand, was definitely not safe.

The year after the Gresham was rebuilt, a young architect called Michael Scott opened a practice in Dublin. He was to become the high priest of the modern movement in Irish architecture. Architectural modernism evolved from nineteenth-century engineering projects and the development of new materials like steel and reinforced concrete. It stressed function over ornament, preferring clean lines and eschewing fussy detail. Scott, as well as other young architects, designed hospitals and cinemas in the new style. These were functional buildings by their very nature, well suited to the plain practicality of modernism.

The outstanding example of early modernism was the terminal building at Dublin Airport, designed in a gentle curve and now a listed building surrounded by what is for the most part dreck. But for all its merits, it was an airport terminal and by definition out of town. Modernism would only announce itself definitively with the building of a great civic public building in the centre of one of the country's cities.

This is why Busáras, Scott's masterpiece, is important. Built between 1946 and 1953, it is the twentieth century's first major contribution to the Dublin skyline. It is not tall, but it is monumental, a pair of rectangles — one slightly higher than the other — set at 90 degrees. It is not as chaste as modernist purists might wish: there is a considerable amount of decoration in mosaic and timber. But what struck the bemused viewers was the sheer amount of glass in the building compared to traditional architecture. In this it was typical of the modern style, although much restrained in that respect compared to buildings to come. Its primary function was as the city's central bus station: the open ground floor serves that purpose. The upper floors are let as offices.

There was, predictably, public opposition. There always is, and modernism in all the arts possesses a shock value that can offend. Public taste often diverges from professional enthusiasm and is generally much more conservative. So it was with Busáras, with objections to the design itself, the scale, the appearance of the building and — always the sure refuge of the irate — the cost. At over £1 million, Busáras *was* expensive but it has since become so secure a part of the city's public furniture that one wonders — as so often with these things — what all the fuss was about in the first place. Just as well there was no talk radio in 1953.

Whether the site was the ideal location for a central bus station is questionable, although its proximity to Connolly Station is an advantage. Access and egress for buses is awkward. What is undeniable is that this fine building has not weathered well, has grown shabby, and is in need of restoration. Plans for such a restoration are in hand at the time of writing.

Michael Scott contributed other buildings to the city, notably the Abbey Theatre (1966), which replaced the old building (see chapter 36) destroyed by fire in 1951. The new Abbey, set on a cramped and unsuitable site, has been less successful and has never won the consistent affection of Dubliners. Busáras is different, dividing opinions to this day but still drawing the praise and celebration of its partisans.

BLASKET CENTRE, DUNQUIN

The first Irish tourist board was established by the new state in 1925. It was not until after World War II that tourism began to make a significant contribution to the Irish economy. Bord Fáilte was established in the 1950s to capitalise on this advance. By the 1960s, the sector had finally taken off in earnest. Income from tourism doubled in that decade alone. Of all the changes wrought by tourism, the transformation in Irish attitudes to food is one of the most noticeable.

It had been well said that Ireland was a good country if you were thirsty and a bad one if you were hungry. Traditionally, the food had been poor: that was putting it kindly. It is sometimes almost an Irish default to blame the English for every misfortune, but this time the charge has some justification. To have been a provincial colony of the European power with the least developed culinary culture was a misfortune. None the less, this hardly excuses the failure to develop a robust native tradition of food in Ireland.

There was no Irish *cuisine paysan*, no tradition of fine cheese-making in a country where dairying was a key part of the rural economy (see chapter 29). Most of all, there was no staple dependence on seafood, this on an island whose surrounding seas were abundant with fish. The Irish fishing industry remained small and expendable: on accession to the EU in the early 1970s, its interests were sacrificed to protect those of the farmers, the more powerful lobby and in truth the more important economic consideration.

One authority has noted that, at the mid-twentieth century, 'cooking styles and taste preferences remained largely conservative and highly repetitive'. Meat, potatoes and two veg reigned supreme, likewise a limited selection of tarts and cakes. Salads were unknown. Bland processed foodstuffs were the norm, yielding a diet that was monotonous and not especially nourishing. Tea was ubiquitous, as in England, but proper coffee was much more elusive. Good restaurants were few and very far between — and altogether absent outside the bigger cities — and eating out, usually in hotel dining rooms whose fare was an extension of the domestic anodyne, was for special occasions. This was the regime that tourism helped to subvert.

The beginnings of the Irish tourist boom coincided with a change of culture in Britain itself. In 1950, Elizabeth David published *Mediterranean Cooking*, which had a profound effect on a country still racked by post-war rationing, a traditional fondness for the 'bit of plain' and an aversion to 'filthy foreign muck'. In time, very slowly, some of these changing British attitudes rubbed off on Ireland, which has never been closed to cultural influence from the larger island.

All this was no sudden revolution. The gradual shift in British attitudes to food coincided with the growing trickle of continental and American tourists to Ireland, demanding better cooking and standards of service. It also coincided with the rise of the first post-revolutionary middle-class generation of Irish people, fascinated by the continent and fixated on getting Ireland into what is now the EU (see chapter 47). Outward-bound tourism helped as well: the growth of the package holiday to the continent from the 1960s onward exposed some Irish people to more adventurous cuisines (or at least to the margins thereof: chips and pies and brown sauce were never far off in resorts popular with Anglophones).

That latter point should remind us that the change in attitudes to food has been partial and incomplete. In Ireland as in Britain it is not difficult to find bad food, badly prepared and served. None the less, the change that has been wrought in the second half of the twentieth century has been little short of transformative. There are few places in Ireland that typify and reflect this better than the little town of Dingle in West Kerry.

It is hardly an exaggeration to say that Dingle in the 1950s was a grey, beaten little place at the edge of the world. It was and is the last town of any size on the most westerly peninsula in Ireland. It had been developed as a port in Norman times, so it has had a continuous urban existence of almost a thousand years. By the mid-twentieth century, however, its population had fallen to barely 1,000 people — although numbers have since recovered. It is surrounded by the most stunning marine scenery. The Dingle Peninsula was made for tourism.

Few places have surfed the tourist wave more successfully. No more grey: almost every building in town has its frontage painted in a bright colour, the contrasts between adjacent buildings aggregating to a cheerful palette. It is an attractive town — and for one whose population is still less than 2,000 people it has three or four excellent restaurants and lots of other good ones. The travel site TripAdvisor lists no fewer than 43 Dingle restaurants, bars and cafés at the time of writing.

In the 1960s, Co. Kerry drew about 100,000 tourists each year. Fifty years later, that figure is more than a million. This has put a huge burden on the county's infrastructure, not least on the Dingle peninsula. There are two main roads to Dingle, neither of them wide: an inland route from the county town, Tralee; and a coastal road along the southern shore of Dingle Bay, with stunning marine vistas. It joins the inland route just west of the village of Anascaul. Current plans to widen and develop this road have raised controversy and opposition. The equally spectacular road to the west of Dingle takes the visitor around Slea Head — more heart-stopping views — and offers the first sight of the Blasket islands.

The Blasket islands occupy a unique place in Irish memory and imagination. The group comprises six larger islands plus some rocky outcrops but all dominated by the

Great Blasket, the largest and most imposing of the group. The island supported a tiny Irish-speaking community, never more than 200 souls, until 1953, when the government felt unable to offer them the state's protection in such a remote and tempestuous location. It removed the remaining population to the mainland. The fame of the islands rests on the survival of this primitive fishing community for so long into the modern era, but more particularly for the three remarkable books written by islanders in the last days of human habitation.

Peig Sayers' *Machnamh Seanamhná / An Old Woman's Reflections*, Muiris Ó Súilleabháin's *Fiche Bliain Ag Fás / Twenty Years A-Growing* and Tomás Ó Criomhthain's *An tOileánach / The Islander* were all first published in the 1930s. The first of these has furnished satirists with rich ammunition for lampoon, rather unfairly, but the other two are masterpieces, especially *The Islander*. Here are the closing lines in the latest English translation, as fine an ending to any book that I know, written by a fisherman who did not learn to write until he was forty:

> Since the first fire was lit on this Island, no one has written about their life here. I'm proud to be the one who did it. This book will tell how the Islanders got on in the old times. My mother was carrying the turf so that she could send me to school when I was eight years of age. I hope to God that she herself and my father will get their reward in the Blessed Kingdom and that I and everyone who reads this book will meet on the Island of Paradise.

Tourism consumes itself, consumes what it sells. In the 1990s, the Blasket Centre was built at Dunquin on the tip of the peninsula facing the islands. It provides the usual tourist experience, retail opportunity and food and drink for the visitors, of whom there are many. It explains, simplifies and interprets the lost world of the Great Blasket. Yet it has offended many by its very presence: the late, brilliant Nuala O'Faolain declared herself 'bullied' by its intrusive presence in this landscape. One can understand this, not because the building itself is offensive. It is not, although no work of genius. Rather, it symbolises what you lose when you surf the tourist wave: reducing an experience so unique that it can best be apprehended through the silence of literature and commodifying it for the amusement of strangers. The food there is excellent.

KNOCK AIRPORT

'The wheels extended. There was a piece of dark bogland and puddles. I could see a straight main road, presumably the Galway–Sligo road, and then, as we passed over it, the small terminal building attached to the control tower, and the long runway. There were conifers behind the perimeter fence. We touched down, turned, and taxied towards the terminal building. Under a large D there was a glass door and people standing behind it had their faces pressed to it. "Isn't it a lovely feeling? I'd never have believed I'd live to see it", a woman said beside me. It reminded me of arriving once at a small airport in Yugoslavia.'

Thus the writer Desmond Fennell arriving in Connacht Airport, more commonly Knock Airport, later Horan International and now officially Ireland West Airport, in the late summer of 1986. Fennell had written a book about Connacht, a work of exceptional shrewdness and merit, and was anxious to dispel all notions of the western province as a lost, benighted place. So instead of crossing the Shannon on foot or by car, he flew in to land in its brand new, bang up-to-date airport.

The driving force behind the building of Knock Airport was the local parish priest, Monsignor James Horan. Indeed, he might be said to have been its onlie begetter. He was a man of remarkable focus and energy, the kind of man who would have been material for a chief executive officer job in the secular world. He had big ideas, confidence in his own judgment, and was a bully and a charmer all at once.

He was not just any old parish priest. His cure was Knock, Co. Mayo, where the Virgin Mary is supposed to have appeared to fifteen local people in 1879. Nor did she come alone: she was attended by St Joseph and St John the Evangelist. The trio positioned itself on the gable wall of the local church, if the testimony of the fifteen were to be believed, which it was by the church authorities. Forthwith, Knock became a Marian shrine and place of pilgrimage.

This was where James Horan first came as a curate in 1963, becoming parish priest four years later. The original church is long gone, replaced a vastly bigger structure suitable to receive the numbers who now attend. Horan oversaw its completion and it opened in 1976. Three years later, Pope John Paul II, another Marian devotee, visited the shrine on the centenary of the apparitions. It was surely Monsignor Horan's apotheosis, this, a visit to his distant parish by the only Pope ever to set foot on Irish soil. One might have thought so, but Horan thought big if he thought anything. He now wanted a regional airport which could service his pilgrimage site and bring energy and employment to a disadvantaged area.

He lobbied, and found a receptive ear. In December 1979, a parliamentary coup in Fianna Fáil, the government party, saw the overthrow of Jack Lynch and the installation of Charles J. Haughey as party leader and Taoiseach. This fascinating, malevolent, corrupt and charming man liked big ideas and liked the men who proposed them. He liked Horan. Moreover, he saw electoral advantage in supporting the airport in a region where Fianna Fáil was traditionally strong. Horan got seed capital of £10 million and the work began in 1981.

Then Haughey's government fell, to be briefly replaced by a coalition of Fine Gael and Labour under Garret FitzGerald, followed even more briefly by a further Haughey FF ministry which collapsed in circumstances of the purest bathos and farce. This time

FG/Lab under FitzGerald was back and stayed in office for nearly five years. The coalition partners had no reason to love Monsignor Horan or his airport.

FitzGerald was an urban liberal, a cool nationalist, a passionate Europhile and an academic economist. He was sneered at as 'Garret the Good' — to contrast him with 'Charlie the Bad', as though 'bad' were a badge of honour — by the journalist John Healy, himself a FF partisan from Mayo. FitzGerald's Labour colleagues had no political presence in Connacht and therefore no electoral interests to defend. The FitzGerald wing of FG and the urban middle-class element in Labour between them represented what passed for social democracy in Ireland at the time; they were emotionally closer to each other — and in truth to some anti-Haughey people in FF — than they were to many in their own parties.

For people such as these, Horan and his ambitions were hateful. An airport in a bog, to service something as embarrassingly peasant as a Marian shrine! And then the huge price ticket for this folly, in a decade of economic crisis and misery. It had to be stopped.

It wasn't. The FG/Lab coalition comprised in disproportionate numbers those elements of the middle class engaged in non-commercial trades and professions: academics, lawyers, teachers and such like. FF had their fair share of these as well, but their heartbeat was close to builders, industrialists and risk-takers in business. FF had a soft spot for a chancer like Horan, pushing his luck; FG/Lab thought he represented exactly the kind of pushy peasant cunning that was half the problem with Ireland.

And what was more, there was all that Marian stuff, all that credulous, ghastly west of Ireland crawthumping, just what we are trying to flee from in the New Ireland! The government called a halt to funding when the project, now well advanced, was only £4 million from completion. It might have thought better to finish it, despite all reservations, on the simple grounds that they were now so far in that it was stupid to get out. But the airport had long got beyond the reach of rational calculation: it was part of a culture war. In this, the age of the farmer — inaugurated some time between the end of the Famine and the 1903 Land Act — was ending. The age of urban bourgeois rectitude was trying to replace it. The urban liberals hated everything about Knock, even the very thought of it.

Horan, to give him his due, bested them all. He raised the greater part of the £4 million shortfall through private donations gathered from home and abroad and the airport opened in 1986. It is still open, more than twenty-five years on. It still receives government grants for capital development and maintenance but no longer draws a Public Service Obligation subsidy. Taking in this support, it appears to fall just short of breaking even in its trading. It retains the continuing financial support of some local businessmen. Its energetic management is trying to develop an industrial zone beside the airport.

There are four airports in the west of Ireland: Shannon, which is losing €8 million a year, Knock, Sligo and Galway. That is arguably three (four?) too many, given dramatically improved road and rail links to the region since the 1980s. The future looks bleak for the latter two. Meanwhile, Knock and Shannon are engaged in what is a zero-sum game for market share of what's left. It is impossible not to admire the sheer chutzpah of the late Monsignor Horan and his supporters. It is equally difficult to argue with the boring good sense of their critics.

EUROPEAN UNION HOUSE, DUBLIN

This perfectly nondescript building stands at the corner of Molesworth Street and Dawson Street in Dublin. It is called European Union House and it is the headquarters of the EU in Ireland. There are similar buildings in every other EU capital.

For the post-1960s generation of politicians and civil servants — and by extension for the socially liberal urban middle class that constituted itself as the new establishment

— Europe was *the* cause of the age. It was the key project of the new bourgeoisie. The chance to drag the Republic of Ireland from its self-imposed isolation, finally to abandon the old Sinn Féin self-sufficiency economics that had brought the country to the brink of ruin in the late 1950s, and to end nonsense like the literary censorship fired the enthusiasm of this new generation. A series of energetic governments led by Seán Lemass, Taoiseach from 1959 to 1966, hitched a belated ride on the post-war capitalist free-trade boom that would continue until the oil shock of 1973. Suddenly, Ireland went from government by gerontocracy to having the youngest cabinet in Europe.

Membership of what was then called the Common Market — now the European Union — was not a necessary condition for this change. But it was its most visible symbol. It gave Ireland a chance to connect with a wider world while by-passing London. Well, almost: for the Irish application for membership was tied to the British application. This was a recognition of economic reality, given Ireland's continuing dependence upon its biggest trading partner. When de Gaulle gave the British application short shrift in 1963, the Irish application died with it.

Eventually, both countries joined in 1972. It was a political decision tempered at first by economic necessity — or perhaps that should be economic reality. Before long, however, political imperatives and psychological desires elbowed economics aside. In the years after independence, Ireland had maintained its currency union with the pound sterling, a union that went back to 1826. It broke this currency union in 1979, launching an independent currency, the punt. This generally traded at a weaker level than sterling, although there were a few giddy moments in the early 1990s when the opposite was true. The punt remained the Irish currency until it was folded into the euro in 2002. The UK retained sterling.

The decision to join the euro was entirely political, as was the euro project itself. As the post-2008 crisis has demonstrated, creating a currency union without a fiscal union and without a central bank that can act as lender of last resort resulted in chaos when the currency was put under stresses that no one had ever anticipated. British Eurosceptics had pointed out these flaws from the beginning, but their objections were dismissed as politically-motivated carping — which indeed they were. Being anti-euro or pro-euro was a political choice. Indeed, not all who criticised the architecture of the common currency were Eurosceptic — far from it, in some cases. Jacques Delors, who had done as much as anyone to drive the European project forward in the 1980s and was a committed supporter of a single currency, had severe reservations right from the beginning.

The Irish commitment to Europe has been an elite project, the property of mainstream politicians, senior bureaucrats, financiers and industrialists — and the farmers, who were in it for the avalanche of cash provided by the Common Agricultural Policy. It has had less purchase among the wider populace. Two referendums to approve EU treaty changes have been voted down at the first time of asking, admittedly on very low turnouts (themselves eloquent testimony of visceral commitment to Europe, or the absence of it). The questions were put again on both occasions and carried on bigger turnouts, the second time to approve the Lisbon Treaty by an electorate thoroughly scared of having to face the post-2008 recession outside the embrace of the EU.

This made some sense, for Irish public finances had run so utterly out of control that without support from the EU the economy might have collapsed altogether. The only alternative would have been some kind of closer connection to the UK and a re-establishment of the currency union with sterling — politically impossible. Once again, politics was trumping economics. For although membership of the EU had brought many advantages — not least by establishing Ireland as an Anglophone base within the Union for the European subsidiaries of US multinationals, especially in the information technology, pharmaceutical and software sectors — the UK remained the country's largest trading partner. True, the level of that dependency had been much reduced over the decades since joining the EU, but the economic link with the UK was still crucial. If economics was the driving motivation, and a currency union was deemed essential, then a re-integration with sterling would have made most sense, or at least a restored punt which shadowed sterling faithfully — which would simply have been a more dishonest version of the same thing.

But the politics of that would have been such an utter humiliation as to be psychologically impossible. One of the ironies of the situation is that the most consistent opponents of the EU have included Sinn Féin, the effects of whose policies would be to bring Ireland closer to Britain, not a position that they normally espouse. While active support for the EU had been shallow, it has been consistent. Principled opposition to it has generally been confined to the likes of Sinn Féin and others on the populist right, attended always by the standing army of useful fools on the far left.

In the 1970s, the Labour Party imagined itself opposed to Europe — and campaigned against endorsing the original entry referendum — but quickly changed its mind. The bourgeois element in the party felt instinctively close to the project, as did the rest of its social class — those easeful liberals whom the Dutch call the *regenten*: the educated haut bourgeois who seem to command the heights of power, whether in office or not. As for the trade unions, their hostility evaporated when they realised that European social democracy offered them greater protections than let-it-rip Anglo-American capitalism.

The two larger parties, Fianna Fáil and Fine Gael — especially the latter, and most especially of all Garret FitzGerald, for whom Europe was almost like a religious cause — never wavered in their support. The effect has been to create a vast elite consensus of the centre and the moderate left around support for the EU. But genuine popular enthusiasm for the Union is lacking in Ireland, as in most other member states. Political legitimacy — the consent to be governed — still resides in the nation state and not in the Union. The democratic deficit in the EU — most visible in the wretchedly low turnouts for elections to the European Parliament — is a tolerable nuisance in good times but is potentially disabling in times of crisis.

DRUMCREE
CHURCH

C o. Armagh is beautiful. There is no other word for it. The back roads, in particular, are a delight, running through undulating orchard country. Yet this small county, at 1,254 sq km the fifth smallest of the thirty-two, is and has been the cockpit of the endless quarrel between Catholic and Protestant in Northern Ireland. It was in Portadown, in the north of the county, that the worst and best-remembered massacre of Protestants took place in 1641, something that no Ulster Protestant forgets for long, if at all. Here, there is little in the way of 'moving on'.

On 4 January 1976, two Catholics were murdered at their farm near Whitecross, towards the south of the county, and another three of their co-religionists died at the hands of loyalist gunmen across the county boundary in Co. Down. The next day, near Kingsmills in the solidly Catholic and republican south of the county, the Republican Action Force (a thinly disguised cover for the local Provisional IRA, which was officially on ceasefire at the time) exacted revenge in one of the most sordid and cynical atrocities of the Troubles — which is saying something.

A minibus carrying sixteen textile workers was heading towards the village of Bessbrook. The men were eleven Protestants and five Catholics, four of whom got off at Whitecross. Near Kingsmills, the van in which the rest were travelling was stopped by armed men. They called the only remaining Catholic forward. Thinking that the men were loyalist paramilitaries, his Protestant colleagues tried to call him back. Instead, he was instructed to leave and not look back, whereupon the eleven Protestant men were gunned down in cold blood. Amazingly, one survived despite taking eighteen bullets. Depressingly, this revenge attack worked — at least for a time. There were no more Protestant murders of Catholics in Co. Armagh that year. The beautiful orchard county lived by its own logic — unforgiving but well understood.

Although a small county, Armagh is densely populated by Irish standards and has been ever since plantation days. Here is one of the clues to its volatility. It is almost exactly the same size as Co. Monaghan adjacent, but has almost two and a half times as many people. The population of Armagh is greater than those of counties Wicklow, Waterford, Kilkenny, Wexford and Clare. In fact, if you exclude Dublin, Antrim and Down, whose figures are distorted by the cities of Dublin and Belfast, Armagh has the third-highest density of population in Ireland, double that of neighbouring Co. Tyrone.

This pressure of population is suggestive. So is its historical distribution. In the eighteenth century, the county had a tripartite confessional division. In the north and east, centred on the linen manufacturing towns of Portadown and Lurgan, the Anglicans were ubiquitous with only a small and marginal Catholic minority. Surprisingly, there was almost no Presbyterian presence in this region. It was confined to a middle buffer zone, running horizontally across the county south of Armagh city. South of that again was a solidly Catholic and Gaelic-speaking area known as The Fews, which ended in the ring of southern hills and drumlins that separate south Ulster from Leinster.

The tensions between these confessional enemies living in such close proximity were not helped by the presence of armed Protestant gangs. The best-known, the Peep o' Day Boys, rampaged across the countryside from the mid 1780s. A Catholic counter-group called the Defenders was centred on the Fews, an area that was relatively remote and introverted. Both sides committed horrible outrages, but the principal volition was on the Protestant side. Competition for land leases may have sparked off the first attacks, but they continued sporadically and violently for a decade and more.

In September 1795, one such affray at a crossroads near Loughgall to the west of Portadown led to the foundation of the Orange Order. The Peep o' Day Boys routed a party of Defenders, killing up to thirty of them. They then celebrated their victory in Loughgall in the house of James Sloan where they founded the Loyal Orange Institution.

The Orange Order has a fair claim to be the most enduring legacy of the 1790s in Ireland. It remains the largest Protestant organisation in Northern Ireland with about 100,000 members and has been a central feature of unionist politics since the 1880s. Its annual parade day, 12 July, celebrates the anniversary of the Battle of the Boyne and is the highlight of the marching season. Orange marches were deliberately provocative and were designed to be. From earliest days, until restrained by an independent Parades Commission established in 1996, they followed traditional routes which made sure to take in Catholic/nationalist areas. This was a primitive marking of territory, a bullying affront to 'the other side' and an assertion of tribal superiority. It was hardly surprising that nationalists wanted Orange marches routed away from their areas and equally unsurprising that the Orangemen resisted.

This issue came to boiling point at Drumcree church, just west of Portadown and only a few miles from Loughgall. Once again, Co. Armagh provided the flashpoint. The Portadown District LOL No. 1, the oldest of all district lodges, held its annual 12 July church service at Drumcree and marched into the centre of the town on a traditional route that took it down the nationalist Garvaghy Road. This had been a source of tension since the late 1970s, but the climax came in 1995 following concerted nationalist protests orchestrated by a Sinn Féin activist and ex-IRA convict. His position as the face of the protest outraged the Orangemen but it reflected the growing self-confidence of nationalists. They simply were not going to be walked over any more.

The police first refused to let the marchers down the road but relented after three days, to the dismay of the residents. Again, in 1996 and 1997, riots and civil disorder accompanied the event but once more the Orangemen got down the road, although their bands stayed silent. In 1998, the Parades Commission finally got hold of the problem and re-routed the march. The price tag had included riots, civil disorder, a huge police and army presence, damage in excess of £10 million and the lowest point in inter-community relations in years, which in Armagh could be a very low point indeed. After the 1996 march, some Catholics organised a boycott of Protestant shops.

The website of Portadown District LOL No. 1 includes an open letter, first published in July 1998 and addressed to 'Dear Fellow Citizens'. It is a remarkable little document and includes the following bromides:

> The disputed parades occur along main arterial roads which are shared by all communities. All are traditional routes, none have been concocted or organised to cause offence. We are not engaged in coat trailing, or triumphalism. We simply want to celebrate our culture and identity peacefully and with dignity.

And later:

> The restricting of loyal order parades along main roads creates cultural apartheid, where one community has a veto on another community's expression of identity and heritage. Banning and re-routing Orange parades from shared road and village main streets will only lead to further segregation of our respective communities. This is not the way to build a future where there is mutual respect and tolerance. Ethnic segregation is morally wrong. It did not work in South Africa and the United States. It must not be allowed to work in Northern Ireland.

This is the first (only?) known instance of the Orange Order invoking fellowship with the anti-apartheid and US civil rights movements.

Not far south of Drumcree, in the Fews — now simply known as south Armagh — the Defender tradition lives on in the form of the most irreconcilable and resourceful IRA district. It was from here that the bomb that nearly killed Margaret Thatcher and half her cabinet came. Some things don't change fundamentally in the beautiful orchard county.

WATERFRONT HALL, BELFAST

F or more than thirty years, the Troubles consumed Northern Ireland. Almost 3,000 people died as a direct result of the conflict. It was a conflict that did no credit to either side. The pettiness and discrimination that characterised unionist rule led eventually to a nationalist revolt. The early unionist response was to repeat the dose of the 1920s: state violence. However, in the television age this proved an embarrassment to the sovereign government in London: the world was able to watch the goings-on in this strange corner of the United Kingdom.

When the civil disturbances of 1969 reduced Northern Ireland to anarchy, the words 'IRA: I Ran Away' appeared on gable walls. The IRA had swung to the left in the 1960s, following the failure of the 1956–62 campaign, and had come under the influence of a Dublin-based socialist leadership. There was a consequent emphasis on social action and lack of emphasis on traditional republican concerns. This proved costly when working-class Catholic ghettos came under attack from loyalist mobs, often aided and abetted by police and B Specials. The movement split. The left-wingers formed the Official IRA and the more traditional — and it must be said more practical — element became the Provisional IRA. The Provos concentrated on community defence in the first instance — to purge the I Ran Away smear — and then moved on to a resumption of the 1920–22 civil war by attempting to shoot and bomb the British out of Ireland altogether.

Following 1969, the police began a rolling series of reforms that, no matter what they did, would never convince nationalists that they were anything other than a sectarian arm of the state. The B Specials were abolished. The local government franchise was reformed to end the sort of gerrymandering that obtained in Derry. It was too little too late.

In August 1971, the unionist government introduced internment without trial. It was a botched job, based in part on faulty and out-of-date security information. But even if it had been a perfect operation, it would have remained a disastrous error of judgment. It massively increased nationalist alienation from the state and support for the Provos, whose operational capacity remained undiminished. The following year, 1972, was the most violent of the troubles, with 470 deaths, over 10,000 shooting incidents and almost 2,000 bomb explosions. In the same year, London closed the parliament at Stormont and imposed direct rule.

The Provisional IRA represented the nationalist extreme. The mainstream was represented by the Social Democratic and Labour Party (SDLP), whose principal theoretician was John Hume from Derry. He preached a reconciliation of the two traditions through negotiation and movement towards an agreed future for both parts of Ireland. The SDLP was totally opposed to the violence of the IRA, not to mention the reciprocated assaults from loyalist paramilitaries.

In 1974, the British and Irish governments and the main Northern Ireland parties reached a deal at Sunningdale, near London, for a power-sharing, devolved government in Belfast. An Executive was duly set up and lasted a mere five months before being brought down by a unionist general strike.

Thereafter, the Troubles rumbled on from one atrocity and ambush to another, with dirty work on both sides and likewise on the part of the British army despite repeated denials which no one believed. The deaths of ten republican hunger strikers in 1981 probably represented a psychological low point, although it also made the more intelligent people in the IRA and Sinn Féin realise that while the war could not be lost it could not be won either. Hunger strike candidates won by-elections and demonstrated the potential for political action. It took the best part of twenty years for this potential to transmute into practical politics. The republican movement was steeped in a culture of violence and would require much subtle persuasion to wean it off the gun. There were practical problems, of which the question of paramilitary prisoners was the most pressing (this consideration also affected loyalist paramilitary groups).

The most important political development of those years was the Anglo-Irish Agreement of 1985, signed by Margaret Thatcher for the UK and Garret FitzGerald for the Republic. It marked the beginning of a genuine *rapprochement* between Dublin and London and increased co-operation between the two governments. Crucially, it set up a joint ministerial conference supported by a permanent secretariat in Belfast. It stopped short of joint authority but gave Dublin a voice in the governance of Northern Ireland for the first time. Although it led to predictable unionist rage at a deal done over their heads, it created the conditions that made the peace process of the late 1990s possible. It also recognised the simple reality that more than one-third of the population of Northern Ireland had no loyalty to the state and had no reason to have any such loyalty.

By the late 1980s, it seemed that the problem of Northern Ireland was insoluble. Here were irreconcilable opposites, renewing an inter-communal quarrel centuries old, speaking and shouting past each other in a dialogue of the deaf. It was a dreary time in a dreary place without much evidence of hope. It was not a time to build. Yet build they did, and splendidly.

The Waterfront Hall in Belfast is the finest concert venue in Ireland, with the possible exception of the Grand Canal Theatre in Dublin. But the latter was designed by the international celebrity architect Daniel Libeskind and was the showy child of the Celtic Tiger. The Waterfront Hall was a local effort, designed by the Belfast practice of Robinson McIlwaine. Planning began in 1989 and the building finally opened in 1997, a year before the Belfast Agreement. In other words, the Troubles were in full swing for most of its gestation.

There was another side to Belfast and to Northern Ireland during all the bad years, and this building is palpable evidence of it. For all its hatreds and horrors, this was not the Balkans or Lebanon. Civil society did not break down. Outside the worst ghetto areas, there was an air of something like normality. Not all of that was illusion. There were strong elements on both sides, not least in the churches, that helped to maintain the common decencies of social life in desperately trying circumstances. For every ranting Protestant ultra like Ian Paisley or for every republican priest, there were heroic figures like Rev. Ken Newell and Fr Denis Faul. One was in no doubt as to their commitment to their respective traditions, but they also gave witness to the best of both traditions — and to their shared Christianity — by refusing to be silenced when they saw evil done by their own side.

They were not alone. History and politics had rendered Northern Ireland an unstable place, incapable of full normality. It wasn't and couldn't be like the Republic or the Home Counties. But considering the stresses of history and of the troubles, corroding the civic fabric of society for so long, the wonder is that it retained as much secular stability as it did. It just did not give up. The peace, when it came, was a fudge; no one pretended that the two sides had suddenly kissed and made up. But it happened, most improbably, when the two political extremes — Paisley's Democratic Unionists and Sinn Féin — somehow contrived an agreement to co-habit and share power in a devolved provincial government. This could not have happened without a civic centre of gravity, a stable middle ground on which the forces of social cohesion could stand. If any building in the province bears witness to these stabilising, normalising forces, it is this.

ST LUKE'S, DUBLIN 9

T his unremarkable red-brick house stands in the suburb of Drumcondra on Dublin's north side. The main road into the city from the airport takes you past the door. Formerly a doctor's surgery, it was bought in 1988 by five close associates of Bertie Ahern TD, the Minister for Labour in the cabinet of Charles J. Haughey.

Ahern was an indefatigable ward-heeling politician in the grand Irish tradition. He had first been elected to the Dáil as a twenty-five-year-old in 1977 and he had built up a formidable personal political machine in the constituency of Dublin Central. Ahern's machine bypassed the official Fianna Fáil party structure in the constituency: it was his creature and existed to promote his political interests and his alone. The team that he gathered round him, including the five trustees of St Luke's, were known simply as the Drumcondra Mafia. They had bought the house to serve as the nerve centre of the Ahern political juggernaut.

Ahern never lost sight of his home parish. He was a local lad from just up the road and no matter how well his political career prospered, he tended his constituency with a single-minded discipline that produced spectacular electoral returns. He consistently drew one of the top personal votes in the city, the bedrock on which everything else stood. And prosper he did, being promoted to the Department of Finance when Albert Reynolds succeeded Haughey as Taoiseach, then succeeding Reynolds as leader of Fianna Fáil and finally winning the 1997 general election. At the age of forty-five, after twenty years in the Dáil, Ahern was Taoiseach.

He contested three general elections as Fianna Fáil leader and won them all. People liked him: he was a nice guy, glad-handing, informal, unaffected. People felt that they could identify with him, that he was more like an Ordinary Joe than most politicians. He was trusted. He assumed the office of Taoiseach as Ireland was in the middle of the most spectacular economic growth in its history. The Irish economy grew dramatically from about 1993 to 2001 by attracting foreign direct investment with tax incentives and furnishing the businesses thus attracted with a flexible and well-educated Anglophone workforce. Ireland became the EU beachhead for some of the United States' best cutting-edge technology companies. Immigrants poured into the country; emigrants returned home. The government had budget surpluses at its disposal. Unemployment fell like a stone. By the turn of the century, GDP per capita was 110 per cent of the EU average, having been at 75 per cent only ten years earlier. Ahern, a football fan, was like a striker who had just received a through pass and faced an open goal.

It seemed he couldn't miss, a view confirmed when he made a critical contribution to securing the Belfast Agreement of 1998, which marked the beginning of the end of the Northern Ireland troubles. This was evidence of Ahern's real gift: he was a brilliant negotiator and conciliator. But like everyone he had the weaknesses of his strengths. He was one to reconcile differences rather than to confront problems. Indeed, conciliation was his default mode, which is one reason why he missed that open goal.

The economic renaissance was wasted. Entry to the euro brought low interest rates and a Niagara of cheap credit. Instead of counter-cyclical measures to stop the economy running out of control, tax breaks, especially for the property sector, flung fuel on the fire. The warning signs were there: even in the real boom of the 1990s, average house prices had more than doubled. They were to double again before the beginning of the crash in 2007. In Dublin, an average house cost the equivalent of €85,000 in 1990; €250,000 in 2001; €420,000 in 2007. Credit card debt quadrupled between 1995 and 2005. In a country getting too relaxed about debt, government policy now helped to replace real productive growth with a debt-fuelled asset bubble.

Powerful interest groups — they exist in all societies, and no politician is immune to their influence — were indulged rather than challenged. And in the carnival atmosphere of the property bubble, few groups were more cosseted than the builders and the bankers. The affinity between Ahern's Fianna Fáil party and the construction industry was of long standing. They were often cut from the same cloth: self-made men of no great sophistication and often little education but energetic, smart, ambitious and adventurous. In a burgeoning property market, they were made men — for as long as it lasted. And it looked, as these things always do, as if it would last for ever. In turn, they were fuelled by the bankers who were their source of credit.

Irish banking had once been a staid old thing. There was a joke that said it operated on the 2, 3, 4 principle: you paid 2 per cent on deposits, charged 3 per cent on overdrafts and went home at 4 o'clock. All that changed gradually from the 1960s on, with the consolidation of a number of small legacy banks into the two pillar banking groups, Bank of Ireland and Allied Irish Bank. But the real change was driven by a maverick outsider, Anglo Irish Bank. It established itself as an aggressive lender in the commercial property sector; it was unstuffy and free-spirited, and it gave personal service and quick answers. It was an entrepreneur's dream bank; it became enormously successful as the property market roared ahead. The older banks, fatally, decided to follow its example and get their slice of the pie.

For the first seven years of the new decade, the Irish banking system went mad. More to the point, it was allowed to. Financial regulation was light to non-existent and warning signs that seemed terribly obvious in hindsight were perfectly invisible while the music played. For instance, rapid balance-sheet growth in a bank is one of the clearest danger signals possible, usually prompting regulatory authorities to force policy corrections on offending institutions. The rule of thumb is that an annual growth rate of 20 per cent puts a bank in the regulator's red zone. Anglo-Irish Bank exceeded this threshold eight times in nine years to 2007. Irish Nationwide, once a little building society and now an aggressive lender in the property sector in the Anglo mould, did so six times in the same period. These were the two financial institutions that were to collapse the Irish economy when the bust came.

Yet nothing was done about them. A culture of light regulation had acquired the potency of a medieval superstition. It was the Anglo-American way, especially since the Reagan-Thatcher revolution, and Ireland was hugely open to this Anglo-Saxon fashion. Moreover, the presence of so many iconic American companies in Ireland — Intel, Dell, Google and others — deepened the American influence. The Progressive Democrat party, the junior coalition partner with Fianna Fáil from 1997 to 2010, had ingested the free market, light regulation menu uncritically and it had a key ally in Charles McCreevy, the Fianna Fáil Finance Minister from 1997 to 2004. In the shorthand of the time, Ireland was closer to Boston than to Berlin.

It was a collective delusion. It is interesting in all-powerful hindsight to see how few 'experts' spotted the coming disaster. All talk was of soft landings in the property market, because markets left to themselves and not interfered with by governments and bureaucrats always self-correct, don't they? Well, they don't, as Keynes had noted. But in the febrile atmosphere of the boom, Keynes was dismissed as old hat. So were the few minatory voices in the land, mere Jeremiahs and spoil-sports. People who might have developed a critical faculty — many of them compromised by employment in errant financial institutions — just did not want to believe that this wonderful party would ever end.

Given that a whole society was in the grip of something larger than itself and was loving it, it was perhaps too much to expect mere politics to offer a corrective. But other societies managed it, notably Canada and Australia, Anglophone countries (for the most part) which did not allow their banks to run out of control and emerged from the world crash of 2008 relatively unscathed. Ireland failed dismally, and the failure must be laid at the door of nice, accommodating, conciliatory Bertie Ahern.

It was the habit of ward politics, nurtured in St Luke's, that made Bertie everyone's friend. The Irish charmer: promising all things to all men, tending the local patch, doing a turn for a fellow if you could, not putting problems in people's way, keeping your friends sweet and having a word for everyone, watching your back, conciliating. Everything except thinking, analysing and acting: that way lay confrontation, and Bertie hated confrontation.

Corrective, regulatory, counter-cyclical policies would not have been popular, and no politician — especially one like Ahern — courts unpopularity. In addition, powerful interests in building and banking would have been ranged viciously against him. Other interest groups, like the public-service trade unions, were similarly indulged in a shameless fraud called benchmarking whereby public servants made material and economic gains in return for efficiencies which were promised but never delivered.

Between 2003 and 2006, while 100,000 jobs were created in the construction sector, the biggest growth of all was in the public service with a whopping 160,000 new positions. Ahern had a care for the unions, who received his serial protection. Having been routed in the private sector, where their presence had diminished almost to vanishing point, the unions were determined to protect their market share among the public-service monopolies.

It was a sad business, the empty-headed and consistent taking of the easy way out. Ahern, the quintessential electoral politician, emptied public life of its content and asserted the unimportance of political thought. Culture matters: the culture of Irish politics, with its ward-heeling and its chummy accommodations, was alive in the shiny new economy and accomplished its destruction.

The culture of localism is as old as Irish democracy and is integral to it. It is an observable constant in Irish public life since the Famine. Because it carries no grand narrative, like the national struggle, and is incremental, discreet and uninterested in theory or ideas, there are times that you could be forgiven for not noticing it. But it is there none the less — and that is how Irish people want it. After the crash, many worthy academics prescribed the reforms that they felt were essential for the revival of political structures. Almost without exception, they recommended a weakening of the PR-STV voting system, precisely because it facilitates localism and parish-pump politics.

There has been little public support for this. People like the system precisely because of what it enables. Elites may hate the petty-minded, down-home grotesques that the system seems designed to throw up, but the electorate unfailingly rewards localism and punishes all TDs who neglect their home patch. It was ever thus. One leading historian of nineteenth-century electoral politics remarked on the central importance of 'the gap between local realities and the rhetoric of national politics'. He added that 'Irish politics … were often profoundly localist both in content and style'. He was writing about the period 1832–85!

Alas, poor Bertie, destroyed by the very tradition of which he was a grandmaster. And alas, poor Ireland, that this is its heart's desire.

BIBLIOGRAPHICAL ESSAY

GENERAL SURVEYS

Thomas Bartlett's *Ireland: a history* (Cambridge 2010) is the most recent complete overview. Like the present work, it ignores the pre-historic past, beginning with the first written documents in the fifth century AD. Jonathan Bardon's *A History of Ireland in 250 Episodes* (Dublin 2008) is based on a BBC Northern Ireland radio series. James Lydon's *The Making of Ireland: from ancient times to the present* (London 1998) has the great merit of being written by one of the country's leading medieval historians, so that his perspective is informed by insights developed in his studies of that period.

Another medievalist, Seán Duffy, has written a useful popular illustrated book entitled *The Concise History of Ireland* (Dublin 2000). For those less inclined to tackle the more demanding academic surveys already mentioned, this is an excellent popular point of departure. The same author is general editor of *Atlas of Irish History 3rd edition* (Dublin 2011). Another fine overview is *The Course of Irish History* (Cork 2001) by T.W. Moody and F.X. Martin, first published in 1966 to mark the fiftieth anniversary of the 1916 rising and continuously updated since.

A.T.Q. Stewart's *The Shape of Irish History* (Belfast 2001) is a lucid short account of fewer than 200 pages written from a unionist perspective. Hugh Kearney's *The British Isles: a history of four nations* (Cambridge 1989) is the work of an Irish historian that places the Irish story in its archipelagic context.

One work worthy of mention is Patrick Corish, *The Irish Catholic Experience: a historical survey* (Dublin 1985), a succinct attempt to do what the author freely admits is an impossible task: to produce an overview of his subject in fewer than 300 pages. Written before the calamities that have engulfed the church in scandal, its conclusions might not be asserted with such confidence today.

An important book comprising thematic essays which addresses what might be called the Irish historical personality is *Inventing the Nation: Ireland* by R.V Comerford (London 2003). The author emphasises non-political issues like language, literature, music and sport.

A number of multi-volume surveys have been attempted and not completed. One that has is the six-volume New Gill History of Ireland (NGHI, 2005–9), itself based on a series first part-published in the 1990s and which in its turn replace a previous eleven-volume series in the 1970s. The individual volumes will be mentioned at the appropriate place in this essay.

OTHER SURVEYS

There have been a number of very distinguished surveys which basically cover the early modern and modern periods. First among them is J.C. Beckett's classic *The Making of Modern Ireland 1603–1923* (London 1966). Written with exceptional elegance and clarity, it gives roughly equal space to the seventeenth, eighteenth and nineteenth centuries, although its conclusion on partition — that it ushered in a period of greater tranquillity than Ireland had known since the 1700s — was to be tragically mocked by events in Northern Ireland within two years of its publication.

Its generational successor was Roy Foster's *Modern Ireland 1600–1972* (London 1988), probably the high-water mark of the so-called revisionist school of Irish history, that is those who challenged the pieties of nationalist historiography under pressure of contemporary events in Northern Ireland. A major work that covers the full span of its subject from the eighteenth century to the present but which is crucial to the period of the Union is Richard English, *Irish Freedom: the history of nationalism in Ireland* (London 2006)

F.S.L. Lyons' *Ireland Since the Famine* (London 1971) has held its place as the best overview of the period 1850 to 1970. Alvin Jackson's *Ireland 1798–1998* (Oxford 1999) and Paul Bew's *Ireland: the politics of enmity 1789–2006* are both compelling overviews, with Bew's work informed by the scepticism of a liberal unionist.

ANCIENT AND MEDIEVAL

The two principal overviews of the Middle Ages are Michael Richter's *Medieval Ireland* (NGHI 1, Dublin 2005) and Dáibhí Ó Cróinín's *Early Medieval Ireland 400–1200* (London 1995), the first volume in a projected series.

EARLY MODERN

The standard survey histories of the sixteenth century are Steven Ellis, *Ireland in the Age of the Tudors: English expansion and the end of Gaelic rule* (London 1998) and Colm Lennon, *Sixteenth-Century Ireland: the incomplete conquest* (NGHI 2, Dublin 1994). For the seventeenth century, Raymond Gillespie, *Seventeenth-Century Ireland: making Ireland modern* (NGHI 3, Dublin 2006) is an interpretative survey from the collapse of Gaelic Ireland to the final triumph of the Protestant interest after Aughrim and the Boyne.

While much of the debate about revisionism in Irish history focused on the modern period, one could argue that Tudor and Stuart Ireland have been the focus of the most outstanding revising scholarship of the past generation. The following is a brief selection of the most important contributions. Nicholas Canny's *Making Ireland British 1580–1650* (Oxford 2001) locates the English plantations in Ireland in a broader Atlantic context. S.J. Connolly's *Contested Island: Ireland 1460–1630* is one of a number of works listed in this essay by a consistently excellent interpretative historian. Hiram Morgan's *Tyrone's Rebellion* (Dublin 1993) is the best history of the Nine Years' War. Similarly, John McCavitt's *The Flight of the Earls* (Dublin 2002) is the outstanding book on the subject.

One of the great classics of Irish historical literature is Edward MacLysaght's *Irish Life in the Seventeenth Century* (rev. ed. 1979) which, although first published in 1939, has stood the test of time in fine style.

For the Cromwellian period, Micheál Ó Siochrú's *God's Executioner: Oliver Cromwell and the conquest of Ireland* (London 2008) has superseded all previous literature on the subject.

THE GEORGIAN ERA

One of the great absences in Irish historical writing was a compelling overview of the eighteenth century. That gap has at last been made good by the publication of Ian McBride's magisterial *Eighteenth-Century Ireland: the isle of slaves* (NGHI4, Dublin 2009). This is one of the very finest works published in the last generation, in a field where the competition is impressively strong.

Toby Barnard, *A New Anatomy of Ireland: the Irish Protestants 1649–1770* (London 2003) is a major study from a major historian. A useful short survey from the same author is his *The Kingdom of Ireland 1641–1760* (Basingstoke 2004). Equal to Barnard in accomplishment is S.J. Connolly's *Religion, Law and Power: the making of Protestant Ireland 1660–1760* (Oxford 1992).

Thomas Bartlett's *The Fall and Rise of the Irish Nation: the Catholic question 1760–1830* is indispensable. Another influential work in this area is Kevin Whelan's *The Tree of Liberty: radicalism, Catholicism and the construction of Irish identity 1760–1830* (Cork 1996).

No mention of the eighteenth century can overlook another classic, Maurice Craig's *Dublin 1660–1860* (Dublin 1980), which, although it overspills the century fore and aft, is firmly anchored in it. The 1790s were the most violent decade in modern Irish history and have prompted an impressive library of published works. Marianne Elliott's *Partners in Revolution: the United Irishmen and France* (London 1982) is a standard background work, as is the same author's *Theobald Wolfe Tone: prophet of Irish independence* (London 1989). Also valuable is Dáire Keogh's *The French Disease: the Catholic Church and radicalism in Ireland 1790–1800* (Dublin 1993). The same author is co-editor with David Dickson and Kevin Whelan of a distinguished collection of essays entitled *The United Irishmen: republicanism, radicalism and rebellion* (Dublin 1993).

For the climactic year of 1798, the only attempt at a synoptic work covering the Leinster, Ulster and Connacht uprisings remains Thomas Pakenham's *The Year of Liberty* (London 1969). That said, its substantial emphasis is on Wexford. Its conclusions and methodology have been challenged by a later generation of scholars and Daniel Gahan's *The People's Rising: Wexford 1798* (Dublin 1995) is now regarded as the most complete account to date of that revolutionary moment. A collection of essays edited by Dáire Keogh and Nicholas Furlong, *The Mighty Wave: the 1798 rebellion in Wexford* (Dublin 1996), broadly endorses Gahan's secular nationalist reading of events. This view is challenged in one of the most intriguing books to emerge from the bi-centenary of 1798, Thomas Dunne's *Rebellions: memoir, memory and 1798* (Dublin 2004), a minor masterpiece. The rebellion in Ulster is the subject of two books by A.T.Q. Stewart, *A Deeper Silence: the hidden roots of the United Irish movement* (London 1993) and *The Summer Soldiers: the 1798 rebellion in Antrim and Down* (Belfast 1995), which reflect an Ulster particularist view of these events.

The risings of 1798 were followed by the Act of Union, the standard modern account of which is Patrick Geoghegan's *The Irish Act of Union: a study in high politics 1798–1801* (Dublin 1999).

IRELAND UNDER THE UNION

D. George Boyce's *Nineteenth-Century Ireland: the search for stability* (NGHI 5, Dublin 2005) surveys the period from the Union to the early 1920s. The same author's *Nationalism in Ireland* (Dublin 1982) is a useful overview. Likewise K. Theodore Hoppen's *Ireland Since 1800: conflict and conformity* (London 1999). The same author's *Elections, Politics and Society in Ireland 1832–1885* (Oxford 1984) is outstanding. Robert Kee's three volumes that constitute *The Green Flag* have been consolidated in a one-volume paperback edition under the same title (London 2000). It is a highly accessible survey of nationalism by a distinguished journalist and historian.

Fergus O'Ferrall's *Catholic Emancipation: Daniel O'Connell and the birth of Irish Democracy 1820–1830* (Dublin 1985) remains the standard work on that decisive event. There are fine biographies of O'Connell by Oliver MacDonagh and Patrick Geoghegan.

The Famine dominates the mid-century and much thereafter. The best synoptic modern account is Christine Kinealy's *That Great Calamity: the Irish Famine 1845–52* (Dublin 1994). The most lasting effect of the Famine was the massive emigration that it triggered, and among the many fine works that emerged from that tragedy few have as powerful a resonance as David Fitzpatrick's *Oceans of Consolation: personal accounts of Irish migration to Australia* (Cork 1994), a book of raw emotional force based on the personal letters of Irish emigrants to the Antipodes.

A book of thematic essays that are genuinely illuminating is Oliver MacDonagh's *States of Mind: a study of the Anglo-Irish conflict 1780–1980* (London 1983). An important political-military survey is Charles Townshend's *Political Violence in Ireland: government and resistance since 1848* (Oxford 1983).

Studies of the nineteenth-century Catholic church are dominated by the work of the Irish-American scholar Emmet Larkin, whose series of seven detailed scholarly studies covering the second half of the century have set the benchmark for all who research and write in this area. Not all of these titles, regrettably, are available outside the United States. An important aspect of church life was its effective control of Catholic education. The book to read in this regard is Barry M. Coldrey's *Faith and Fatherland: the Christian Brothers and the development of Irish nationalism 1838–1921* (Dublin 1988).

The era of Parnell, from the 1870s to his death in 1891, was dominated by the twin questions of land and nation. Paul Bew's *Land and the National Question 1858–82* (Dublin 1978) makes this connection explicitly. Alvin Jackson's synoptic *Home Rule: an Irish history 1800–2000* (London 2003) is useful, as is Philip Bull's *Land Politics and Nationalism: a study of the Irish land question* (Dublin 1996). That key group, the Fenians, have at last got the scholarly notice they deserve thanks to Owen McGee's *The IRB: the Irish Republican Brotherhood from the Land League to Sinn Féin* (Dublin 2005).

In the welter of books about the revolutionary period, there is only room to mention a few. Conor Cruise O'Brien's *States of Ireland* (London 1972) is, like just about everything O'Brien wrote, a compound of disguised autobiography, history and polemic, but its interpretation of Irish public life from the fall of Parnell to the outbreak of the Northern Ireland Troubles influenced a generation as few books have done. The standard work on the greatest labour dispute in Irish history is Pádraig Yeates's *Lockout: Dublin 1913* (Dublin 2000). The three best books on the 1916 rising are Charles Townshend's *Easter 1916: the Irish rebellion* (London 2005), Fearghal McGarry's *The Rising: Easter 1916* and Max Caulfield's *The Easter Rebellion* (Dublin 1995), a re-issue of a work first published in 1964. It had the great advantage that the author was able to interview survivors of the rising.

Arthur Mitchell's *Revolutionary Government in Ireland: Dáil Éireann 1919–22* (Dublin

1995) tells of the remarkable parallel civil and legal administration that Sinn Féin put in place as British power declined in nationalist Ireland.

The best account of the Anglo-Irish treaty negotiations remains Frank Pakenham's *Peace by Ordeal* (London 1935). Michael Hopkinson has produced the two standard works on the 1919–23 period: *The Irish War of Independence* (Dublin 2002) and *Green Against Green: the Irish civil war* (Dublin 1988).

ULSTER

One of the very finest books to emerge from the Troubles was the travel writer Dervla Murphy's *A Place Apart* (London 1978). Taking the hint from her title, I have concentrated the books relating to Ulster and Northern Ireland in this section.

The standard history of the province, and one of very best books published in Ireland in a generation, is Jonathan Bardon's *A History of Ulster* (Belfast 1992), a marvellous *tour d'horizon* that runs from the Mesolithic Age to the 1990s, just before the apparent permafrost of the conflict began to thaw. Thomas Hennessey's *A History of Northern Ireland 1920–1996* (Dublin 1997) explains itself. The distinguished journalist Susan McKay's *Northern Protestants: an unsettled people* (Belfast 2000) is an 'insider's' account of the community that formed her, although she has long since settled in the Republic. Counterpointing her are Marianne Elliott's *The Catholics of Ulster: a history* (London 2000) and Oliver P. Rafferty's *Catholicism in Ulster 1603–1983: an interpretative history 1603–1983* (Dublin 1994). An important work, often overlooked, is Peter Brooke's *Ulster Presbyterianism: the historical perspective 1610–1970* (Dublin 1987).

A.T.Q. Stewart's *The Ulster Crisis* (London 1967) is a compelling and sympathetic account of unionist opposition to home rule in the years before the Great War. The same author's *The Narrow Ground: aspects of Ulster 1609–1969* (rev. ed., London 1986) is a deeply influential book originally published at the outset of the Troubles. Its interpretation of Ulster particularism was troubling for nationalists.

There are many accounts of the Troubles themselves and of the IRA but the best, as it seems to me, is Richard English's *Armed Struggle: the history of the IRA* (London 2004). David McKittrick and David McVea's *Making Sense of the Troubles* (London 2001) is a lucid account. The British journalist Peter Taylor has written two insightful books, one each about the 'two sides': *Loyalists* (London 2000) and *Provos: the IRA and Sinn Féin* (London 1998). Finally, Paul Bew and Gordon Gillespie's *Northern Ireland: a chronology of the Troubles 1968–1999* (Dublin 1999) is part reference work, part extended essay and in any event essential.

THE REPUBLIC

Dermot Keogh's *Twentieth-Century Ireland: nation and state* (NGHI 6, Dublin 2005) belies its title by virtually ignoring the North, for which the reader must look to Hennessey (above). But as an account of how the newly independent state, soon to be the Republic of Ireland, established and consolidated itself, it is excellent. By contrast with Keogh, Henry Patterson's *Ireland Since 1939: the persistence of conflict* (Dublin 2006) does straddle the border although — perhaps inevitably given the long shadow of the Troubles — it gives more space to the North than to the Republic.

J.J. Lee's crackling *Ireland 1912–1985* (Cambridge 1990) and Diarmaid Ferriter's *The Transformation of Ireland 1900–2000* (London 2004) are the most complete surveys of the twentieth century. Terence Brown's *Ireland: a social and cultural history 1922–2001* (rev. ed., London 2010) is an update of a classic survey first published in the 1980s.

Irish neutrality during World War II has produced a rich literature that does much to explain the political culture of the new state. Robert Fisk's *In Time of War: Ireland, Ulster and the price of neutrality* (London 1983) was instantly hailed as a classic. Three more recent books are worth noting. Brian Girvin's *The Emergency: neutral Ireland 1939–45* (London 2006) argues that neutrality was against the national interest and scuppered the chance of attaining a united Ireland, not a reading that everyone will agree with. Claire Wills' *That Neutral Island: a cultural history of Ireland during the Second World War* (London 2007) is the work of a literary critic who brings her skills to bear on the Irish cultural elite and on neglected sources such as provincial newspapers in a genuinely original approach.

The post-war period is well covered in the general surveys noted earlier but two books deserve special mention here. John H. Whyte's *Church and State in Modern Ireland 1923–79* (Dublin 1980) was the second edition of a work that had first appeared ten years earlier. It remains the best and most level-headed account of twentieth-century Ireland's key institution, the Catholic church, and its relationship to the new state. Tom Garvin's *Preventing the Future: why was Ireland so poor for so long?* (Dublin 2004) answers the question posed in the sub-title with characteristic brio.

The literature covering the second half of the twentieth century in the Republic is not especially rich, inevitably overshadowed by the northern Troubles. But the Celtic Tiger boom, followed tragically by the property bubble, produced first a crackerjack celebration of the good times. David McWilliams' *The Pope's Children: Ireland's new elite* (Dublin 2005) was the exuberant work of an economist turned journalist with an enviable talent for analysing and explaining arcane economics in a lucid and compelling manner. Nor was he a mere cheerleader: at a time when few wanted to listen, he was one of a tiny band who warned of trouble ahead. When the crash did come in 2008, it produced a torrent of books on how the country had got itself into this mess. Most were focused on economic analysis or narrative of one kind or another: there was no shortage of material. Fintan O'Toole's *Ship of Fools: how stupidity and corruption sank the Celtic Tiger* (London 2009) is the best social and cultural analysis.

PHOTO CREDITS

For permission to reproduce photographs, the author and publisher gratefully acknowledge the following:

© Alamy: 1, 13, 19, 42, 50, 64, 65, 68, 76, 79, 87, 99, 101, 103, 106, 109, 114, 121, 125, 143, 151, 174; © Collins Photo Agency: 170, 182; © Corbis: 4, 17, 27, 128, 155, 178; © Department of the Environment, Community and Local Government: 162; © Ger Lacey: 88; © Getty Images: 7, 10, 16, 21, 30, 34, 37, 38, 41, 45, 54, 71, 72, 80, 84, 92; © Imagefile: 53, 82; © Inpho: 147, 149; © Irish Times: 166; © Michael Diggin: 24; © Mike Searle: 46, 49; © Peter Zoeller: 140; © Photocall Ireland: 57; © RTÉ Stills Library: 159; Courtesy of Ireland West Airport Knock: 169; Courtesy of the National Library of Ireland: 96, 110, 118, 132, 136; Reproduced with the permission of Trinity College Dublin: 61.

INDEX